WE ARE ALL
SELF-EMPLOYED

**The biggest mistake you can make is
to believe that you work for someone else.**

—*H. Jackson Brown*, The Father's Book of Wisdom

WE ARE ALL SELF-EMPLOYED

The New Social Contract
for Working in a Changed World

Cliff Hakim

Berrett-Koehler Publishers
San Francisco

Berrett-Koehler Publishers, Inc.
155 Montgomery St.
San Francisco, CA 94104-4109
Tel: 415-288-0260   Fax: 415-362-2512

ORDERING INFORMATION
Individual sales. Berrett-Koehler publications are available through bookstores. They
can also be ordered direct from Berrett-Koehler at the address above.

Quantity sales. Berrett-Koehler publications are available on quantity purchases by
corporations, associations, and others. For details, contact the "Special Sales
Department" at the Berrett-Koehler address above.

Orders for college textbook/course adoption use. Please contact Berrett-Koehler
Publishers at the address above.

Orders by U.S. trade bookstores and wholesalers. Please contact Publishers
Group West, 4065 Hollis St., Box 8843, Emeryville, CA 94662; tel. 510-658-3453;
1-800-788-3123; fax 510-658-1834.

Printed in the United States of America

Printed on acid-free and recycled paper that is composed
of 85 percent recovered fiber, including 15 percent post-
consumer waste.

Library of Congress Cataloging-in-Publication Data
Hakim, Cliff, 1951–
    We are all self-employed : the new social contract for working in a changed
world / Cliff Hakim.
        p. cm.
    Includes bibliographical references and index.
    ISBN 1–881052–79–6 (alk. paper)
    1. Psychology, Industrial. 2. Work--Psychological aspects. 3. Employee motivation.
4. Job satisfaction. I. Title.
HF5548.8.H23 1994
158.7--dc20   94-21708
                                                                 CIP

First Hardcover Edition: August 1994
99 98 97 96 95 94   10 9 8 7 6 5 4 3 2 1

First Paperback Edition: September 1995
99 98 97 96 95   10 9 8 7 6 5 4 3 2 1

TO AMY, for stretching, listening, loving, and being part

of my journey; **TO MY MOTHER**, for teaching me,

"When everything seems lost, you always have yourself";

and **TO MY FATHER**, for reminding me,

"It's another day; make the most of it."

Contents

Preface

This book is not about starting your own business. Then again, it *is*, for its intent is to challenge and influence your beliefs—the ways you think about and do your work. "We are all self-employed" is an empowering belief that you can use to steer your direction and influence the quality of your life. "We are all self-employed," whether we work in an organization—CEO, vice-president, manager, staff member—or outside an organization—consultant, supplier, entrepreneur. This idea may at first strike you as farfetched. But in today's world, your individual, authentic contribution, ability to collaborate with a team, and capacity to produce are more important than ever. Doing your job *and* going beyond it— beyond blind loyalty to any one organization or to your career, trade, and customers—may be a new concept to some of you, but it can reap enormous rewards, personally and professionally.

Individuals and organizations—IBM, General Motors, Xerox—are undergoing extraordinary change. People are losing their jobs, questioning their careers, redefining their identities, consolidating their debts, expanding their options, and shifting their loyalties. Organizations are "laying off," doing more with fewer employees, building self-directed work teams, and buying services from a growing contingent: a part-time workforce. Many workers, regardless of their level or industry, are learning that they must begin to think and act carefully and openly as the world restructures and as they grow personally. The old foundation is gone. People are looking for a new anchor, a "personal anchor," in a transformed job market. *We Are All Self-Employed* explores what it means to practice a "self-employed" attitude and how to make it work for you.

Thinking of yourself as self-employed is an attitude that says, "I am a business partner; I have integrity and a responsibility for working *with* the organization and the customer and for attending to my own personal and professional development." The idea that we are all self-employed is the truth about us and a statement about our changing and challenging world of work. It is not a selfish truth but a liberating one—a philosophy for success.

This book is designed to free you to be your best, most authentic self and to share your best work so that you can use your skills and aptitudes, express your values, and feel you are making a worthwhile contribution. I encourage you to be creative and to take action—to deepen and expand your way of thinking and being and to pursue your goals. *We Are All Self-Employed* supports your passion and integrity. Your passion is your spirit—your deep interests and values, your inner core. From here spring ideas and the energy to commit to meaningful action. Your integrity—who you are and what you believe—is your power and security in a less predictable, more competitive world. I hope this book will help you to build the bridge between managing practical tasks—paying the bills—and expressing passion and maintaining integrity in your life.

Why I Wrote This Book

I wrote this book primarily to take people from merely surviving to fully succeeding. Surviving—continually making adjustments to a shifting culture, a downsizing organization, or a demanding customer—can turn us into androids: robotic, unfulfilled, angry human beings who make mechanistic, routine changes simply to *adapt* to environmental conditions. Instead, you can act courageously by contributing *your* ideas and actions rather than accepting mine or others' at face value.

Surviving = Adapting

Succeeding = Creating

In my practice as a career consultant, I have worked with many professionals, at all levels, in the fields of sales, law, human resources, engineering, finance, and others. I wrote this book to reach a broad audience and to support those of you who have already begun your journey to make sense of personal and global changes. As you reconcile and determine what you bring—skills, values, desires, passion— and what you *want* to bring, you will undoubtedly contribute to your workplace and to a marketplace of dynamic change.

Why Read This Book?

Read this book if . . .

you have the desire to reawaken your spirit and overcome your fear of change. For most of us, it is not enough merely to survive—to change according to other people's desires or to get by on a day-to-day basis. Rather, I believe, we want to go beyond survival, not only to awaken our "inner core" but also to live our passion, express our spirit, and make worthwhile contributions. When we are "self-employed," we are not cogs on a wheel, cared for by the organization, but individuals responsible for our own job productivity, career mobility, and career fulfillment. With self-knowledge, we can better identify our needs and values, build a sense of mission into our work lives, and contribute more to others.

you are interested in stimulating dialogue about healthy work. Those of you who want to take control of your career and whose job it is to envision new directions and influence others have an obligation to yourself, staff members, and customers to speak and act from the truth. Healthy work occurs when you are able not only to work collaboratively with others toward a common goal but also to maintain a clear sense of self and your own goals. Without a clear sense of self, working effectively with others is not possible.

you want to share what you have learned with your friends and your children. Your children are inheriting a different and challenging world. In some ways, they have no choice but to initially accept the new work world. They will also learn ways to use their imagination, skills, and energy for thinking productively, for promoting and managing change, and for enjoying their work. Your clarity, integrity, and activity will inspire them.

I tell my children all the time, "If you are lucky enough to see what the right thing is for you, do it."

—John Shibley, director of training and development, L. L. Bean

Read this book if . . .

you wish to live a fuller life, feeling good about every stage while continuing to contribute to the lives of others. If you live with a "self-employed" attitude, you might say, "Work is *part* of my life, not all."

you are already thinking and acting with a "self-employed" attitude—learning about yourself, overcoming your fears, partnering with a team, and doing meaningful work. *We Are All Self-Employed* will support your learning, independence and interdependence, creativity, and beliefs. It will also offer you challenging and stimulating ways to build on your current skills and promote even greater depth and ingenuity.

A New Social Contract

Dependence on the organization is obsolete. The familiar employee-employer contract has now been broken. Loyalty to the organization no longer guarantees job security. Workplaces en masse are reshaping themselves to survive and compete, and millions of individuals have lost their jobs. You may have lost your job or, no doubt, you know someone who has. Today, and for the foreseeable future, people's employability lies in their own hands.

This book espouses a new social contract: that we are all self-employed inside and outside of organizations. Independence—striving to know and rely on one's self—and interdependence—the ability to collaborate with others, are the contract's core elements. We are no longer entitled to our work, but must earn our jobs by developing ourselves and serving customers; simply completing tasks is not enough. This idea puts a tremendous amount of responsibility on individual workers—CEOs through staff—to make decisions about their personal and professional development, and how they collaborate with others to do their work.

Emerging from disorder, equality and mutual respect are the current order. The new social contract—ecumenical in nature—involves and affects every worker and organization, and demands flexibility and creativity.

About the Quotations

Several of the quotations used in this book are derived from a massive networking effort. I talked with people I knew and with many others I didn't know and asked them to share their thoughts and stories about the notion that we are all self-employed. Many of the quotations are "golden nuggets," and I hope they prove useful to you.

Special Notes

Throughout this book, I use the term *worker* rather than *employee* because *employee* feels and sounds subservient to me. We are all "workers" no matter what we do, working with organizations that are becoming more horizontal and crossfunctional. Our focus needs to be on contribution and initiation, not on subservience—the suppression of self and ideas.

With the exception of the cases in chapter 6, I have used pseudonyms to honor individual and organizational client confidentiality.

Each chapter begins with an illustration of the sprial. The spiral is the universal symbol for evolution and growth. It is associated with the need for change. A "self-employed" attitude fosters growth and supports change.

How This Book Is Organized

The Introduction compares an "employed" with a "self-employed" attitude, presenting and clarifying therein the minimum critical requirements for you to develop and sustain a self-employed attitude. Individually, the subsequent six chapters form the essential building blocks for *embracing* a self-employed attitude; collectively, they provide a powerful transformational system for *living* this attitude. The exercises in each chapter will deepen your understanding of a self-employed attitude. On page 20 the themes of the chapters are united into six beliefs that constitute a "working creed."

Cambridge, Massachusetts   Cliff Hakim

June 1994

Acknowledgments

This book is a manifestation of my personal work life and beliefs. Ever since I was a child, my gut instincts have known that we are all self-employed, that none of us really works for anyone else. I am indebted to many people who, throughout my life, have participated in my learning and to those who have made this book possible.

I'd like to thank my family for their spirit and encouragement; the people who agreed to be interviewed and helped me to refine and clarify the concept "we are all self-employed"; those people discussed in chapter 6, who shared their stories with me and agreed to share them with you; and my clients, both individual and organizational, from whom I learn every day.

I am grateful to Steven Piersanti, president of Berrett-Koehler Publishers, for his passion, dedication, guidance, and vision, and to the Berrett-Koehler team—Patricia Anderson, marketing director; Val Barth, publicity manager; Robin Donovan, promotions manager; Valerie McOuat, director of business and administration; Kristen Scheel, sales manager; Mark Carsten, trade sales manager; Elizabeth Swenson, production director; and Liz Paulus, office manager—for their individual expertise and collective support of this project. I'd like to thank the Berrett-Koehler organization for its work on this planet: "opening up new space" by helping others rethink their job, their career, and their organization.

I'd also like to thank the following people for their thoughtful insights, helpful support, and invaluable feedback: Mark Campbell,

Roger Drumm, Marvis Wilson, Jennifer Myers, Patricia E. Barrett, K. L. Murrell, and Stephen E. Forrer.

My gratitude to Ralph Katz for his heartfelt guidance and insightful and expert comments; he lives the principles in this book.

My special thanks to Deborah Sosin, my writing consultant and coach, for her wisdom, encouragement, teaching, questions, and technical expertise.

My appreciation to Roberta H. Winston, my editorial consultant, for her invaluable contribution—ensuring clarity of expression and consistency of voice, time, and style.

All the people who have generously contributed their insights and expertise to the writing of this book are committed to deepening their "self-employed" attitudes, sharing their commitment, and passing on their knowledge to you.

Introduction

From an Employed to a Self-Employed Atittude

"Self-employment" has been both a work concept and an activity throughout our history, but few of us have acknowledged it. For most, the notion of self-employment has remained undercover, hidden behind the so-called employee-employer contract and behind our misconception that we are employees, working for and protected by organizations. In contrast, independence and interdependence, not dependence, are at the core of the new social contract.

More than twenty years ago, Richard Bolles, author of *What Color Is Your Parachute?*, told us that we didn't have to be constrained by traditional job titles or prescribed career paths. We each, according to Bolles, were in effect self-employed—able to identify our skills, uncover hidden opportunities, create and develop more challenging and rewarding work, sell ourselves to various organizations, and serve our customers. For years we have ignored this message, favoring instead the drive toward prosperity and opportunity. Organizations are now recognizing that the worker-employer contract has changed. However, while *they* may not fully believe the notion "we are all self-employed," *we* as individuals have a choice either to believe it or to be forced into it. Why? Because the reshaped global economy is forcing workers, organizations, and cultures to reevaluate themselves.

Thousands of organizations worldwide are engaged in a process of *re*developing. They are *re*defining, *re*planning, *re*vitalizing, *re*orienting, and *re*training to develop *re*freshed selves. They are *re*acknowledging, *re*capitulating, and *re*adjusting to global forces and trying to become more efficient, productive, and competitive. Organizations are learning and *re*learning to navigate against constantly shifting tides. The waves of world competition are crashing against the door of every organization. Maintaining the traditional employment contract against such forces has become too costly. Instead, organizations and developing businesses are recognizing or are forced, like you, to reevaluate what they need to succeed and survive.

Burning the Grass

Way back when, in the late summer or early fall of each year, my grandfather would set his lawn on fire. We called it "burning the grass," and he believed it made the lawn come back greener and richer. The neighbors called it crazy, and eventually the fire department put a stop to it. As a child of seven or eight, I was curious and sometimes confused. I wasn't sure whether to believe my grandfather or the neighbors. But as the years passed, I accepted my grandfather's ritual as a means of producing something better. Even though others saw it as chaos, I learned that my grandfather knew what he was doing: The grass always grew back greener.

In the employment arena, what looks like chaos can actually be a vital part of change and growth: learning a new profession or taking a new job. The process requires moving through chaos—anxiety, confusion, resistance, and aloneness—in the interest of assembling the many disjointed, misunderstood, and often unrecognizable pieces. It is a time of reaching inward and of self-learning. It is a time of reflection, observation, idea generation, and renewal. And it is a time that is central to all people who examine their "employed" attitude and choose to learn a "self-employed" attitude.

As my grandfather burned the grass, I learned not to judge what I saw even if others did. I stood back, watched, and appreciated that *something was going on that I may not have understood at the moment.* If I was patient, I just might notice something valuable. Now I look back at "burning the grass" as a metaphor for my grandfather's life and possibly many of ours—especially during these times. My grandfather's message was, "Look back through the years; you can learn from them. Pause, get perspective, then do what you think is right. Respect your wisdom. You *can* make a difference."

If we are open to learning, history and our own wisdom can be great teachers. Many of our forebears were "self-employed" workers; they burned the grass. Eventually, workers learned to believe that those who owned their own companies were self-employed, whereas people who worked for organizations were not self-employed; instead, they were entitled to their jobs, benefits, and perks. The urgent message of this book is that an "employed" attitude is no longer an option today. You can adopt a "self-employed" attitude—you can choose to burn the grass. You can assimilate a new social contract—independence and interdependence.

Why People Moved from Self-Employment to Working for Others

- Nationally, the economy underwent a shift from farming to factory work and manufacturing.

- Members of the same nationality sought to work and live in homogeneous communities.

- Decisions were usually left to the boss.

- Income was available to meet the needs of people's consumer lifestyles.

- Social needs were partially met.

- Working for others offered more consistency and less volatility than self-employment.

Self-employment—individuals working the land—led to "being employed" by large organizations—independent pioneers and settlers working for others. Individuality—the freedom to burn the grass—was traded for "the good life" or the hope for it. I doubt most people understood what the price would be; nor, in many cases, did they have a choice. I believe my grandfather understood. Even as he prospered—built a home, bought a car, acquired rental property, sold parcels of land—*he* raised crops. Although he never said so, I know that farming the land was a source of his strength, his inner harmony. He prospered in the "new" world and respected the "old" world. He tended to his family, to the earth, *and* to himself.

Like a fast-moving locomotive, the industrial machine was changing the landscape and the people. The capitalistic landscape influenced people's decisions to work, primarily in the factory. People learned to depend on organizations, in a sense, and traded their individuality for mechanistic routines of production so as to earn a living and buy goods and services. They gave up "control" over their lives—their creativity—and let the organization become their identity. The following section addresses specific types of workers and applies the concept of "self-employment" to each.

Man is not the creature of circumstances.
Circumstances are the creatures of men.

—Benjamin Disraeli

You Can Live a "Self-Employed" Attitude

People in every conceivable contemporary work situation—company worker, business owner, part-time worker—or stage of their career—

unchallenged, laid-off, early-retired or never-want-to-retire, recent college graduate—can live a "self-employed" attitude.

If you are a . . .

company worker, your job is not an entitlement or a subsidy. The company is not responsible for you. It cannot be—it has its own pressures and best interests in mind. Nobody cares more about you than you. Dependence is a black hole for all workers. Can we expect companies to have our best interests in mind? Aren't we all responsible for ourselves and for communicating with our customers? Interdependence requires that you constantly organize your work life to do things in a different way. Many variables are not in your control, but a great many are. You can work *as though* you are working for yourself—doing what you do best *and* satisfying your customers. Have you thought of taking the perspective of being a perpetual learner? Be prepared, personally and professionally.

business owner, who defines for you what your business is about, clarifies who your customers or clients are, or shows you how you can remain competitive? You must attend to your personal and professional growth, identify how your customers are changing, and market only what they will buy from you. Everything you do is a reflection of you and your business. You have to be better and do more than you did yesterday. Every day is a challenge.

part-time worker, you have to be willing to invest yourself every day. You are providing your wisdom, skills, values, and creativity, working as a team player with a customer. Is it enough just to put in time? Your customers know their business better than you do. Do you ask them for information and apply what *you do best* to meet their needs? Do you identify first what people need and then offer them your solutions? Every customer is a recipient of what you have learned from former customers. Don't let anybody, including yourself, tell you that you don't have a "real" (full-time) job.

unchallenged worker, admit you are unchallenged. Have you asked yourself why? What would challenge you? It is time for self-assessment, not necessarily with the goal of leaving your company or customer. Here is one perspective: You are paid to solve problems and continue to be paid to solve problems, including your own. Are you aware that it's natural to plateau in your job? Develop some healthy skepticism about what you have to offer. You may be unable or unwilling to take your skills and broker them. If you can't or don't want to, you'll need to develop a plan and learn new skills. Whatever you do, assess, plan, and act. Get out of your joyless rut. It's your life—claim it!

laid-off worker, this is part of your job continuum—and a productive field in fallow times. Give yourself time to grieve your loss. Vent your anger, but only with people you trust. This can also be a precious time, a time to get to know yourself, learn what you have to add to the marketplace, and discover what others will buy from you. Give yourself permission to learn and question what you believe and what you value. Do you feel confused more often than not? Be receptive to others' opinions, but do not lose yourself in the process; appreciate your skills and experience; integrate your aptitudes—your natural talents—into your work; ask and struggle with your questions; persevere until you find the answers; create imaginative alternatives; decide what to do and deal with the consequences; and recognize your successes. Get out there and ask more questions. Stay the course—it's a marathon, not a sprint.[1]

early-retired or never-want-to-retire worker, focus on what you want to do. That's first. Find support for and build an "I can create work" or "I can add value" attitude. You have your wisdom and know-how to give to the world. Why would customers trust you? Maybe they are looking for answers and believe you can solve their problem! Have you researched and learned everything you can about what interests you? Actively network and gather information. You know many people, and those people know many others whom you should get to know. Build a bridge—a business or job—between your skills and the needs of the marketplace as uncovered through your research.

recent college graduate, the job marketplace is a new place of learning. Consider each experience a fantastic graduate education; take what you learn from each and apply it to your next encounter. The process, especially of finding your first job, may not happen in the way you thought it would or be what you thought it would be. Select a challenge that interests you. Have you looked for role models and mentors who are doing what you want to be doing? It isn't easy, but it's worth it. Continue to learn about yourself and the world of work. Build relationships, be flexible, persevere, *give back*, make yourself an expert, and say thank you.

Dependence Is a Black Hole for All Workers

Whatever your work situation or stage of career, this book shows you how to manifest a "self-employed" attitude. The following chart compares an "employed" attitude and its practical applications with a "self-employed" attitude and its practical applications. The word *attitude* implies that each of us has the ability to learn and make choices about how we work and live. If you choose to live a "self-employed" attitude, you will feel inner security, achieve your goals, and contribute the best parts of yourself in an unpredictable, formidable world.

▞

Comparison of an Employed
with a Self-Employed Attitude

"Employed" Attitude *Dependent Mindset*	*Practical Application*
My employer or customers will change in ways that will benefit me; they are to blame if things don't work out.	My boss is all wrong. My customers don't know what is good for them. They'll eventually see things as I do.
If I just put my head down and work harder I'll be safe. I can ignore my fears of knowing myself, losing my job, or understanding my passion.	After all I've done for them, they can't fire me.
I am dependent on the company/customer. They know what I do best and what is best for me. They will take care of *me*.	Whatever job offer I get, I'll take.
I am enmeshed with the company/customer; I work for them. Whether I agree or not, I do what is expected of me.	I sit attentively listening to what my boss or the group needs and then do it.
I can hold on to my successes and be satisfied. If I can only get what I want—position, title, benefits—then I can rest on my past accomplishments.	I know the politics enough to stay safe.
What I do doesn't really matter. I'm just doing a job. I bring my body to work and leave my spirit behind.	My job is boring; there is nothing new to learn.

"Self-Employed" Attitude *Independent and Interdependent Mindset*	*Practical Application*
I will begin the process of change with myself; career self-management is my responsibility.	With a career counselor's help, I am able to assess my skills and values and to focus on priorities at work.
I will face the dragon—my work fears—and replace fear with passion. I will share my ideas, identify my skills, values, and desires, and ask questions to clarify my focus both for myself and my company.	I'll talk with trusted colleagues to clarify company goals and to determine where best to focus my energy.
I will integrate independence and interdependence. I will strive to be myself and collaborate with others.	When I interview, I'll present what I have to offer, ask about what the organization needs, and assess if the job is right for me.
I will join, not work for, my organization and customers. I provide a service based on equality and competence, whether I work in or outside the organization.	In a meeting, I listen and contribute my thoughts.
I will commit to continuous learning, personal growth, and gaining new perspectives. My career is a lifetime endeavor. My mistakes and successes lead to expanded thinking and further contribution.	I ask questions to determine my customers' needs and then make the necessary adjustments in service.
I will create meaningful work. I am resourceful and able to give value to my work—market my skills and negotiate for my needs—and make a contribution regardless of my job or level.	I ask questions, take in feedback, sell my ideas, and try to meet a tangible goal at least once a week.

Each of the six "self-employed" beliefs is the subject of a chapter; each is talked about and illustrated in detail. Collectively, they form a strong spine, supple and supportive, for leaving the mindset of dependence—the black hole—behind. Like the human spine, if one vertebra is out of alignment, we feel pain and our posture suffers. As you read this book, it will help you to refer back to the six "self-employed" beliefs at different times and make it your goal to work toward their ultimate alignment—the healthy work attitude.

Why Choose a Self-Employed Atittude?

The following pages explore why the six beliefs that comprise a "self-employed" attitude are critical in the current work climate.

1. I Will Begin the Process of Change with Myself

It's a new era. The global economy, the great equalizer, is here to stay. The cold war has ended, the military is demobilizing, and Third World countries have become economic powers. With this new world reorder (disorder!), corporations are no longer safe bastions for chief executives or any other workers.

Many full-time workers are receiving reduced benefits, and the part-time workforce, from blue-collar to professional, is growing tremendously. A controller, for example, who had been working at one company full-time, is now working part-time with two, three, or four clients. He commented, "After a long period of self-examination, I have decided to become a part-time controller and business consultant." He provides business and financial support for small- to medium-size businesses.

In the past, the company cocoon provided a secure place, with income, benefits, title, advancement, identity, and stability. The cocoon protected the workers' identities while they waited for retirement or even for death. "We are all self-employed" changes the way we view our entire lives. "It's very scary to me sometimes. It takes time to assimilate," says Jean Bonney, director, External Research Program, at Digital Equipment Corporation. "Eighty percent of the time, I say I want to take command. For the other 20 percent, I'm still scared. Everybody has got to come to the point of being their own change agent."

Expecting that your employer and customers will continue to change is realistic, but expecting that they will change in ways that will benefit *you* is not. Marshaling your own resources—skills, values, aptitudes, and creativity—would increase your control of your job productivity and career mobility regardless of external circumstances. The dependent mindset—that is, hoping others will do the changing and then blaming others for what doesn't work for you—gives others your power and leaves you stuck in unsatisfying situations.

2. I Will Face the Dragon—My Work Fears

At a March 1993 lecture at Harvard University sponsored by the Association for Part-Time Workers, guest speaker Dr. Harris Sussman, strategic consultant, opened by saying, "We are all self-employed." He reported that the fastest-growing group of workers consists of people working *from* home. These people, who work at all levels in diverse occupations—accounting, real estate management, financial planning, sales, publishing—are connected to other individuals and organizations via telephone, fax, and computers. Charles Handy writes, "By some estimates, one-quarter of the working population will be working from home by the end of the century. From home is different than at home. The home is a base, not a prison."[2]

We live in an era of multiple work alternatives: full-time, part-time, telecommuting (working from home via computer, fax, and phone), and job sharing. If you tend to be afraid because times have changed and will continue to change, it will be harder for you to see the virtue of alternatives and to take action. The majority of clients I've seen over the past ten years are working differently today from how they did in the past. Generally, they overcame their fears of change through self-examination and deliberate action. Some who worked full-time now work part-time, others who worked in large corporations now work from home, and still others have left their profession to pursue an avocation as their source of income. Change can liberate people from situations—positions and titles—that no longer work. The clients mentioned above overcame their central fear: that if they let go of what they knew, they would land in a permanent, cavernous void. Freed from their title, fears, and fixed expectations, they tapped into their personal resources and sought work that fit their needs for personal growth and the needs of the organizations and customers with whom they worked.

◪

**The environment is too unstable to promise a future.
We have been forced to betray the mid-century contract that if
you work hard and deliver, we will take care of you.
We need to create a workplace that evokes commitment
that is not based in false promise.**

—*Peter Block,* Stewardship: Choosing Service over Self-Interest

3. I Will Integrate Independence and Interdependence

This book results from a combination of both my thoughts and the reactions, responses, and stories I gathered in person or by telephone from working people across the United States—people from government, education, large corporations, small businesses, and nonprofit associations. When I talked with people about the notion that we are all self-employed, I was amazed to discover the numbers of people who reacted positively. Some said, "That's it!" Others said, "Imagine if numbers of people in companies could learn to think this way." Some responded, "I think this way, but I've never mentioned it to anyone else." My question invariably evoked a visceral reaction. Although some didn't have all the words to explain their response, people seemed to have an understanding that we are all self-employed. They wanted to know what others had to say.

I began each interview by asking, "When I say, 'We are all self-employed,' what does this mean to you?" Most often, the initial response was "Responsibility." Curiosity led to inquiry. I then asked, "What does responsibility mean?"

The word *responsibility* captures the central theme of this book. It is the ability to act independently *and* interdependently—to be your authentic self, collaborate with others, and work productively. We live in a world where self-leadership—taking responsibility for knowing yourself and for engaging in deliberate thought and contribution—is increasingly becoming a virtue. It is a choice to go beyond survival to success. Dependence, the other choice, is a capitulation to your fears, and it will always hold you back from reaching your potential. Layoffs, unchallenging work, and demotions won't go away by burying them.

**In a word, each man is questioned by life;
and he can only answer to life by answering
for his own life; to life he can only respond
by being responsible.**

—*Viktor E. Frankl,* Man's Search for Meaning

4. I Will Join, Not Work for, My Organization and Customers

An organization can no longer guarantee a worker at any level long-term employment. A plant construction manager, for example, working with a *Fortune* 500 computer manufacturer, had been rewarded for building several advanced technical manufacturing plants, but in recent years his employer had been consolidating those facilities. The manager had no control over the shifting, shrinking market, and despite his accomplishments he lost his job.

As organizations are being forced to reinvent themselves, so too is our whole culture. Workers are now without guarantees of "expected" job safety nets—benefits, long-term employment, bonuses, and career advancement opportunities. The organization has always been loyal to its own success and survival. Are you loyal to your own success?

Carole Hyatt, market and social behavior researcher and author of *Shifting Gears* and *When Smart People Fail*, helps put the concept of "joining, not working for" in perspective. In an interview, she said, "There is no such thing as lifetime employment, but there is lifetime employability. We are all doing piecemeal work. We are working in structures of adhocracies as opposed to within the structures of bureaucracies. As adhocracies we supply to bureaucracies; we act and work as an adjunct to organizations." Realistically, we temporarily supply our expertise to a customer: the organization and its customers. Whether or not they see it or believe it, engineers at such companies as Data General, Digital, and Microsoft, for example, are ad hoc to the organization, supplying their expertise in developing state-of-the-art technology. They will have work for as long as the organization needs them or for as long as they feel their work is suited to them. Nurses, in a similar way, are ad hoc to the health care facilities where they work. They will have work for as long as the organization needs them or for as long as their needs are being met. This arrangement is not without its price, but if workers choose to move to another organization—that is, customer— they will be ad hoc to the new organization as well.

None of us can afford to return to massive parental, hierarchical organizations that have closed mentalities. Instead, as Margy Hill, bro-ker-owner of Re-Max Classic Real Estate, said, we are moving to "a great reflowering of our entrepreneurial spirits. You can take control of your life. It is painful, but it's extraordinarily rewarding." Currently, organizations are flattening—that is, running with fewer levels and people, utilizing more advanced technologies, and buying one anoth-er's core competencies. The boss, so to speak, is learning to share and collaborate with experts: you. And workers are learning what Barry Orenstein, senior market research associate with Blue Cross and Blue Shield, has learned: "I'm more of a salesman these days, consciously selling myself, cultivating relationships, and tuning in to how I can serve and meet the needs of people in the organization."

5. I Will Commit to Continuous Learning

We all work two jobs—one of them is being our own career self-man-ager. Continuous learning is the central qualification for this job. Why continuous learning? Because learning is your only guarantee now for developing new insights, perspectives, solutions, and actions.

"How can anyone work two jobs? One is demanding enough," you might respond. What follows is a job description; like any job descrip-tion, this is a "working" one, one you will need to change as you and your organization or workplace changes. At the moment, try not to decide whether you would apply for or accept this job. First read the description:

Job Description

Workers, Inc.

Job: Career Self-Manager

Hours: Between two and four hours per week

Location: Flexible—at an office or at home, in your car, on the beach, or at your favorite coffee shop

Process: Self-paced

Summary: You must be able to take responsibility for your own career mobility and job productivity while making a contribution to the organization and customers.

Qualifications: Any worker, at any level, in any profession, can apply for this job. We encourage inquiries and your application at any time. We anticipate a continuous flow of openings, whatever economic conditions exist. This career self-manager position will require that you take the initiative for career planning, for negotiating with management for self-development needs, and for recognizing ways in which you can add value to the organization and customers.

You must be able to . . .

- describe how things have changed in the marketplace, in your place of work, and in your job.

- discuss your concerns about loss, transition, and managing change.

- assess your individual responsibility and how much you can control in your job, with your customers, and in your organization.

- discuss the benefits of moving in multiple directions, not just vertically up the ladder.

- feel good about asking for and getting the support you need.

- clarify and prioritize your values.

- identify your skills and decide which are most meaningful to you and which are most marketable to others.

- develop "action-results" or "results-action" statements and learn how to use them effectively.

≣ examine your beliefs and determine which are barriers to growth and which are catalysts.

≣ develop one to three specific career goals and a professional development plan that includes a realistic time line for meeting these goals.

Salary: This is a permanent growth position. You can expect to begin earning approximately the same amount that you currently earn. Your earnings may fluctuate depending on your profession, your ability to negotiate, your workplace, and marketplace conditions. We recommend, whether you decide to take this job or not, that you save as much money as possible and invest wisely in order to build a financial cushion for sustaining and advancing your career.

Philosophical Statement: We are all self-employed—inside and outside of organizations.

Values Statement: Working in our changing world requires authenticity, collaboration, and productivity. We must know ourselves as individuals—emotionally, intellectually, spiritually—distinct from our "employed" identity. With this self-knowledge, we can better identify our needs and values, build a sense of mission into our work lives, and contribute more to others.

Many of you are "out straight," trying to keep up with your job or lack of one, as well as meeting family, social, and community obligations. To take on the job of career self-manager along with your other responsibilities may seem daunting. Yet this new job is a growing, flexible, evolving commitment, not another straitjacket that restricts you to rigid hours and routines. The description is a message and a guide to encourage you to take part in a process of learning about who you are and about changes and opportunities in your workplace and the marketplace. You and others who take on this job will most likely want to rewrite the description as you grow and as external conditions warrant.

⊠

**The only sustainable competitive advantage
for individuals is their ability to learn.**

*—Stew Stokes, Jr., senior vice-president,
QED Information Sciences, Inc.*

6. I Will Create Meaningful Work

As a boy, I worked landscaping yards and painting houses. This job
meant I could work in the glorious outdoors. I made my own schedule,
found my own customers (some found me), and made my own decisions. My general goal was to improve and maintain property and to
develop my techniques. Thus, I consciously gave meaning to my work.
The more meaning I gave it, the more I felt thankful to have it. I
embraced with deliberate thought and action what *appeared* routine to
others. I learned, for example, to select the right paint or plants for particular conditions. My "self-employed" attitude was taking shape back
then. Creating meaningful work can increase self-esteem and enthusiasm, attract customers and rewards, and open up new opportunities.

No work inherently possesses meaning. You develop a "self-
employed" attitude by using your power to give meaning to your work.
Only you can give meaning to your work, and only you can take it
away. Deliberate thought and action create a gateway to sustaining
meaning in your work. No matter what you do, creating this gateway
and using your creative resources to develop meaning in your work
are up to you. Even in the supposedly high-status professions—medicine, law, accounting—the rumblings of change are turning into large
noises. "I saw medicine very traditionally. You open up an office or
join a group practice and someone else takes care of billing, paper-

work, and marketing," remarked Mark Haberman, an internist. "This is no longer true," he continued. "Today we must master the business skills, including supervising others, as well as our medical skills. We have an opportunity to gain control of our employment destiny, leading to greater creative control and ideas. But we have to ride out social, economic, and psychological waves in order to keep our head above water. All of a sudden, we are thrust into the business world. We must overcome our resistance and master new skills." For many, overcoming resistance and mastering new skills constitute the entrance to meaningful work.

The Learning Process

The diverse people who have contributed to this book have learned or are in the process of learning that if they don't operate from their passion, they will always be afraid.

There will always be layoffs, downsizings, shifts in the economy, and so forth. When these events influence *you*, your fear may be appropriate, but it does *not* have to dictate your actions. Fear won't dominate you if you know your assets and values. Instead, you'll be able to evaluate situations and make the best choices. The people who have contributed to this book endured their struggles, conquered their external obstacles, and sought innovative ways of harnessing their abilities and clarifying their own and others' needs.

It is important consciously to choose to *live* the six beliefs, a choice between an "employed" and a "self-employed" attitude. To take responsibility for your job productivity and career mobility while serving others is a *lifetime* endeavor. As you engage in this process, you'll need to learn and *integrate* the six beliefs, which are summarized in the "working creed" that follows.

We Are All Self-Employed
A Working Creed

I will begin the process of change with myself.
Start with my own personal growth

I will face the dragon—my work fears.
Replace fear with passion

I will integrate independence and interdependence.
Be myself and collaborate with others

I will join, not work for, my organization and customers.
Build work and work relationships based on equality and competence

I will commit to continuous learning.
View my career as a lifetime endeavor

I will create meaningful work.
*Work, believing that the world offers what I need
and that I can make a contribution*

BEGINNING THE PROCESS OF CHANGE WITH YOURSELF

Start with your own personal growth

This chapter begins to compare in more depth an "employed" with a "self-employed" attitude. A complete list of these attitudes appears on pages 8–9. As you read each chapter, refer back to the comparison list as a guide toward "self-employment," the healthy work attitude.

EMPLOYED ATTITUDE

Dependent Mindset

My employer or customers will change in ways that will benefit me; they are to blame if things don't work out.

SELF-EMPLOYED ATTITUDE

Independent and Interdependent Mindset

I will begin the process of change with myself; career self-management is my responsibility.

O N A TRIP TO NANTUCKET, a quaint Cape Cod island off the coast of Massachusetts, I met Josh, a world traveler. Josh had been to the Near and Far East, Africa, Europe, South America, and a variety of islands. As he was telling me about his journeys, he pointed past a knoll and proclaimed, "Over there, that's the house I grew up in." I said, "You've returned home?" I'll always remember Josh's response: "I tried to find the answers outside of me. Traveling taught me that change begins at home."

Living a "self-employed" attitude begins at home—with you. Insight—knowing yourself—and deliberate hard work—planning and taking action—are the basis of personal change and inner security. Josh traveled the world seeking an answer; his question was, "What do I want to do for work?" "I realized," Josh said, "that traveling didn't give me the answer. In retrospect, traveling was part of my answer. The other, more significant part was an internal journey—the adventure of knowing myself, of coming back home." Through soul-searching, courage, perseverance, and his knowledge of the world, Josh found his answer: adventure. And he has since become a foreign diplomat.

I asked Josh what he would recommend to others who decide to embark on a journey of personal growth and discovery. He offered five suggestions:

1. Remind and encourage yourself, continuously, that you can change and feel better about and more productive in your life.

2. Take time every week to think about what you are doing and learning. If you are so inclined, keep a journal.

3. Find people to talk with—a friend, spouse, counselor, or support group—about your feelings, concerns, and aspirations.

4. At least every three or four months, take a look at your goals and ask yourself, "What do I need to learn to achieve them?" Develop a plan and take action.

5. View confusion and fear as normal parts of your growth; working through them takes courage and will lead to clarity and success.

The chart on the next page gives an overview of the work world today and builds on what Josh had to say by suggesting some guidelines to consider as you navigate toward a "self-employed" attitude.

Personal Redeveloping

"Personal redeveloping" is the harnessing of your creativity, abilities, beliefs, thoughts, and actions in order to rethink, redefine, and reconstruct your job or career to achieve fulfillment and productivity. In my work with organizations and individuals, it has become clear that as organizations redevelop the way they work, individuals too—as was true of Josh—are becoming more responsible for learning the concepts and tools for managing change.

Personal redeveloping is a gradual, endogenous process that requires ongoing growth from the inside of you outward. The *Oxford American Dictionary* defines *developing* as "making or becoming fuller or more mature." Personal redeveloping involves discovering and rediscovering your personal knowledge and applying it in order to control and use your power.

Achieving results through personal redeveloping can be complex and confusing. The process is rarely linear. There was a time when

The Changing Work World

The Work World	You, as Self-Employed
Reality: Organizations have changed and will continue to change.	You must change too.
Financial and extrinsic rewards used to be more plentiful.	Balance internal and external rewards.
The worker-organization contract has changed.	Know and be loyal to yourself.
Hiring is done selectively.	Research specific opportunities thoroughly and do your "inner work"—self-research.
Managerial opportunities are fewer.	Create work and explore personally satisfying niches.
The market is productivity-driven.	Know how you can add value.
Organizations have become flatter.	Develop *in* your job; climbing the ladder is not the only option.
Full-time employment has become only one form of work.	Part-time work, consulting, job sharing, and telecommuting are options.
Workplaces are redeveloping, task-oriented, learning environments.	Personally develop and grow, affirm your purpose, and contribute.

achieving and advancing in one's work seemed more straightforward and when certain accomplishments all but guaranteed particular results. Teachers graduated with their master's degree and headed directly for an opening in a public school; new MBAs were recruited by and had a choice of working at several Wall Street investment banks; diligent supervisors could expect to be promoted to manager. External conditions aligned, clearing paths for relatively unfettered career advancement and recognition.

To ease the pain, reduce the complexity, and streamline the personal redeveloping process, I ask individuals to focus on the three questions that follow. You can apply these same three questions to realize and harness your power, whether or not you work in or outside an organization or are in career transition.

1. **What do you want?** Do you want to bake bread or sell houses? Do you want to act in plays or write scripts? Do you want to use your persuasive abilities to practice law or raise funds? Do you want to design computer technology or consult with customers on how to use the latest technology, or both?

2. **What do you bring?** What skills, experiences, values, ideas, and personal qualities do you offer? How can you derive personal satisfaction as you bring these parts of yourself to your work?

3. **What will others buy?** Is what you want to do worth a purchase price? Why would your company or a customer pay you for what you do or sell?

These questions work best when you view them as a constellation, akin to a group of stars; their grouping, not one alone, creates the design. You can develop a new career opportunity for yourself by answering all three questions and putting those answers into action. But because things don't always work the way we think they will, let the questions sit. Don't rush the answers. Often when my clients are looking for a career change and they come up with their first potential job option—an "answer"—I say, "Good first step. Now let's look at why you think this might fit *and* at other possibilities." Together, we sit back, generate new ideas, and evaluate what we have. The best answer(s) will emerge through a combination of examination and serendipity.

Streamlining Personal Redevelopment

What do I want?

What do I have to bring?   What will others buy?

Wild Horses

Rollo May, consulting psychologist, says, "To use Plato's time-honored figure, there are in the unconscious a number of horses straining at the bit to be off in different directions."[1] I frequently say to clients, "Your work is to harness the wild horses—personal qualities, skills, feelings—running around inside of you so that you can manage change, align your resources, and progress toward your goal." Naming and harnessing the wild horses is a metaphor for personal redeveloping. The questions, "What do you want?" "What do you bring?" and "What will others buy?" are your guides—the harnesses.

Realigning the Wild Horses

Lisa was multitalented but unfulfilled. Over the span of her career, she had worked in the areas of counseling, teaching, proposal writing, public relations, drama, and administration. When Lisa sought consultation on career and work issues, she was an editor in a large publishing firm. She was also at a point of desperation, feeling that her work fundamentally had little meaning or interest. Time was passing her by, and she complained, "I have done so many things and done them well, but I've never been happy at any of my jobs. I don't know where I'm headed."

Together, we explored the range of her feelings—fear, anger, hopelessness—and identified other obstacles to her finding career satisfaction. I asked Lisa to clarify her skills and strengths using a tool called "Harness Your Wild Horses." She used this tool as a vivid metaphor to develop a "self-employed" attitude and achieve her career goals. First, she listed all her positive personal and professional qualities and how she wanted to use them in a work setting. Her list included thoughtfulness, curiosity, creativity, and empathy. During the course of several sessions, I helped Lisa to name her skills: writing, creating, analyzing, and synthesizing. I encouraged her to imagine that each of her skills represented a wild horse that was confined within a fenced-in area. What would happen if the gate were simply opened? All the wild horses would scatter in different directions. But what if each of these horses were harnessed? Their energy would be focused, and they would be unrestrained to move forward freely and joyfully.

Lisa's "team of wild horses" was now metaphorically harnessed. This technique effectively helped her to move forward in reality. She unearthed a longtime goal of being a scriptwriter and, over a period of four months, with occasional coaching sessions for guidance and encouragement, launched a job search with renewed energy and a positive outlook.

The question remained, "Could she get paid in this role?" Her inner harnessing created energy that led to a focused networking effort. She discovered a scriptwriting position in her company's video department, where she now works.

Reframing as a Tool

Reframing transforms meaning and behavior: A rock becomes a paper-weight—you place it rather than throw it. A piece of fruit becomes decorative art—you notice its contour but refrain from taking a bite. A puddle you jumped over becomes a mirror you now look into. Your impatience becomes your desire to achieve. You step back, clarify your goal, and focus your energies.

You can reframe thinking of yourself as "employed" to thinking of yourself as "self-employed." Rather than waiting for others to tell you what to do, for example, take the initiative to begin a new project.

After expressing anger about and grieving her demotion, one client, Andrea, reframed her situation as a time to learn as much as she could about herself and her work options. She wrote a note to me: "The time of job loss is painful but also very precious in the sense that it allows/forces people to discover." As Andrea learned about herself and about career options, she got to the point of seeing her boss as a catalyst and felt she would never have discovered these other dimensions had she remained in the same job. A *de*motion, in her eyes, became a *pro*-motion. Lisa, the editor, reframed her background. She harnessed her wild horses and focused her energy to become a scriptwriter. Both Andrea and Lisa thought about things differently and discovered a means to create new possibilities in their lives.

Organizations also reframe themselves. The formerly giant IBM, for example, has split into smaller, more manageable entities. AT&T has transformed itself from a telephone company into a communications network and service. Insurance companies and banks, such as John Hancock and Citicorp, have reframed themselves, becoming financial service providers. And US West, a phone company, "aims to turn its 14-state network into a so-called broadband super-highway to consumers and businesses."[2] Reframing affords success and survival not only to individuals but to organizations as well.

Just as redeveloping can reframe an organization, so too can personal redeveloping help you to see things differently and to work through internal and external obstacles as you go about harnessing your wild horses. You may discover that the skills you want to use are too specific or out of date, that your expectations of the organization no longer fit with the workplace reality, or that you have difficulty focusing on one or two options. These examples and others are found on the next page, "Reframing Your Career Mobility."

Reframing "Career"

"Career defined me," proclaimed Mara, a city planner. " 'City planner,' " that's who I *was*. No matter what—snowstorm or sick child—I'd go to work. Now, some years later, I've learned there are other parts of me; my job is only one part." Richard, an engineer and professor, said, "Career for me means to be productive—an inherent need to be productive." And Toby, a consultant, commented, "I don't think in terms of career but in terms of my skills. My job is applying my skills to a company's needs."

"Career," for some people, is what defines them; for others, it is an active state; and for many, it has meant and will continue to mean following a specific course or an occupation, such as a career in law or engineering. As you grow and the reality of the workplace shifts,

Reframing Your Career Mobility

The following examples show how some of my clients have reframed their behavior to achieve their career goals.

Current Situation *What's Going on Now*	Reframe *New Viewpoint*
I'm arrogant.	I'm self-confident.
I'm impatient.	I like to get things done.
I'm a poor leader.	I'm an excellent individual contributor and team player.
I have difficulty closing off options.	I'm flexible. I ask others to help with the final decision.
I'm too aggressive.	I'm determined.
My skills are too specific.	I'm a problem solver and fast learner. As the company changes, I can contribute and adapt.
I feel discouraged.	I need a rest.
I'll take any job.	I'm ready to focus on three options.
I've been told I'll never make the switch from nonprofit to profit or manufacturing to service.	This change may not happen in a single move. Instead, I'll work on a project or part-time basis.
I'm not getting anywhere. I haven't received a raise this year.	It's time to regroup and reward myself. I'm going to demonstrate how I can add value. Then I'll propose a compensation range based on my research.

reframing can be an invaluable tool. Career *could* mean choosing a variety of jobs or projects in which you utilize your evolving skills, values, aptitudes, and interests to create a lifetime of adventure and contribution. Think about what career means to you and begin writing your thoughts, as in this sample sentence:

For me, career is one of the highest forms of self-expression. Through my career, I contribute to others and feel good about myself.

There Is No One to Blame

Blame has no place in the process of personal redeveloping. Blaming the boss for not getting a promotion, blaming the customer for not buying the product, or blaming the competitive job market for not getting the job will hold you back from learning what you need to learn in order to progress to your next goal. Blame creates judgment that interferes with learning and growth. You stay stuck. One client, Andy, a forty-six-year-old investment analyst, spent years hoping that his firm would recognize his ability to work effectively with customers. The recognition never came. Fed up, Andy left the firm, blaming its managers for their lack of attention and recognition. Shortly thereafter, he returned to school to study counseling psychology. Now Andy laments, "I've wasted time and money. School feels like an unreal world to me, and I miss the business world. I can't believe I made such a poor decision at my age."

Before he left his job, Andy had believed the firm would change in ways that would benefit him. When he decided to go to school, he grabbed the first opportunity that would satisfy his need to be in a people-oriented profession. In both situations, Andy blamed others for his unhappiness, lack of insight, and inability to represent himself.

With some coaching, Andy realized in hindsight that he could have built on his experience at the firm and sold himself into a position that more fully represented his abilities and interests.

Don't Blame, Reframe

After six years at the same hospital, Wendy, a pediatrician, inadvertently discovered that her salary was much lower than that of her colleagues. She was angry, and her initial reaction was to call me and say, "I've been treated unfairly, and I need to start looking for a job elsewhere. I don't think I'll be able to get a raise. Will you help me plan a job search?" After evaluating her options, Wendy began to see that she might experience the same inequity at any other facility she might join. Then what would she do?

She told me she was afraid of being rejected if she asked for a salary increase. I encouraged her to talk about her fear and, as she did, she discovered that her plan for immediate action was precipitous. A better plan would involve using one of her best skills—research—to uncover information about what other pediatricians were earning in similar situations, in and outside the hospital, *before* she acted. In addition, to reaffirm her abilities and contributions, she took an "inventory" of her skills and accomplishments. (This process will be discussed later.) Researching what others were earning, taking an inventory of her skills and accomplishments, and organizing her thoughts helped her to view her current situation more clearly. Informed now, not driven by anger or fear, she could enter into negotiations with increased self-confidence.

Wendy made a significant strategical and philosophical decision: She reframed, looking at her situation *as if* she were self-employed. She did her research and clarified her value to the hospital. Then she scheduled an appointment with the manager of her unit to "discuss an important business matter." Prior to the meeting, we role-played possible scenarios. In the actual meeting, she presented her case calmly, offered her research for review, and, after a period of negotiation, received a salary increase.

Up Is Not the Only Way: Reframing the Career Ladder

Question: How does a career ladder fit in flattening organizations?
Answer: For the majority, it doesn't.

Latitude is necessary in flattening organizations. People need to make decisions flexibly, move to where problems need to be solved, and get the work done. When organizational growth appeared boundless, the system took responsibility for the workers' upward mobility, pushing them up to the ladder's next rung. As organizations grew, workers learned to expect advancement; the organization would take care of them. Today's flatter organizations can no longer support hundreds of people climbing their career ladders or motivate workers in the traditional fashion. This is the new reality—the career lattice.

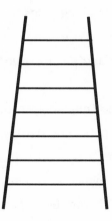

Career Ladder

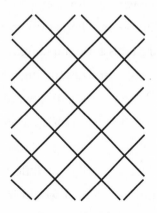

Career Lattice

A career ladder suggests that there are only three ways to go: up, down, or falling off. Up usually means success; going down or falling off . . . well, most of us try to avoid these.

By contrast, the career lattice is a viable alternative for career mobility and job productivity, for its structure supports different paths, each one involving career choices based on skills, values, interests, competition, workplace and customer needs, and individual and group initiative. A career lattice provides many options that a career ladder cannot. Douglas, for example, worked his way up the ladder to become a partner in a public relations firm. As partner, his role changed from direct consulting with clients to managing workers. But as the marketplace changed, he needed to lay off staff and step off the ladder. Douglas became a consultant again, moving in any direction—that is, using the career lattice—so that customers would be served and the firm would succeed.

Career-ladder thinking brainwashes us to compete with others for more pay, more prestige, more visibility, and fewer jobs up the ladder. Competing alone can divert us from focusing on our jobs. On the other hand, the career lattice, as Douglas discovered, affords different ways to think and act, thereby increasing opportunity and opening passageways for contribution. Career-lattice thinking helps us concentrate on excelling at our work and delivering service. These are necessary tools for competing in the marketplace and for discovering work that is personally and organizationally valued.

The career lattice would support a junior engineer in his or her efforts to contribute to a project without the person necessarily moving "up" into another position. Rather than being rewarded with a title— which typically has little to do with performance in a dynamic culture—the person would instead be rewarded with the opportunity to contribute and learn, with the *possibility* of earning more money by meeting mutually defined goals.

For a senior engineer, for example, the career lattice would encourage her or him to mentor a junior worker and gain knowledge of new systems design and customer needs. The rewards could include recognition for developing others' potential, financial remuneration (compensation aligned with the flatter system), and the learning of new, marketable skills. When appropriate, both junior- and senior-level engineers could also be encouraged to rewrite their job descriptions and create new job titles. These changes would more accurately account for and reflect their growth and the needs of the organization and the customer.

Career-Ladder Thinking	*Career-Lattice Thinking*
Movement is restricted—up or down.	Movement is at any angle—up, down, or from side to side.
Promotions are most important. Titles are revered.	What and how workers contribute are most important.
The system is autocratic—the boss has the answers.	The system is collaborative—"let's see what we can figure out."
Static, short-term strategy is used—promotions are temporary.	Fluid, long-term strategy is used—"we encourage you to grow with us."
Expertise exists at the top of the ladder.	Expertise exists companywide.
Rewards are based on loyalty and title.	Rewards are based on learning, contribution, and performance.
Much internal competition with others exists, sometimes at the expense of the organization and customers.	External factors are considered, and competitive goals are set by the worker.
Workers are dependent on others for self-worth.	Independence, flexibility, and teamwork are fostered.

Career-ladder thinking—positioning workers for upward advancement—makes less and less sense. The cornerstone of career-lattice thinking is self-management, encouraging workers to take control of their own careers. Career-lattice thinking means creating a shared vision that embraces career mobility for the individual and a competitive advantage for the organization.

This diagram is representative of the traditional career ladder in an organization. Compare it with the career-lattice diagram shown below it.

Career Ladder

Vice-president of engineering (one)

Manager of engineering (one of two)

Senior engineering product manager (one of nine)

Engineering project manager (one of seventeen)

Associate engineer (one of twenty-five)

Junior engineer (one of fifty)

Career Ladder: Up is the *only* way to advance.

Career Lattice

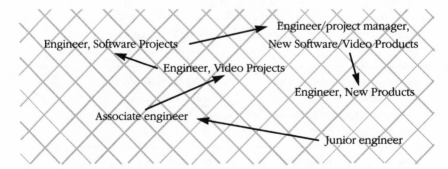

Engineer, Software Projects

Engineer/project manager, New Software/Video Products

Engineer, Video Projects

Engineer, New Products

Associate engineer

Junior engineer

Multiple Roles
(Engineer, Software Products)

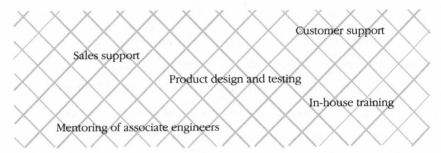

Customer support

Sales support

Product design and testing

In-house training

Mentoring of associate engineers

Career Lattice: Job mobility and multiple roles are possible for more workers.

Don't Look Up

The linear path of climbing the career ladder represents a false security. I check the *Wall Street Journal* daily to get a sense of the job scene. On Tuesday, August 24, 1993, the *Journal* reported, "Layoffs outstrip the pace set in recession year 1991. . . . With IBM's recent big layoff announcement, 1993 furloughs are averaging 50,516 monthly, topping 1991 by more than 4,000 a month." Climbing the tidy ladder may have been effective when organizational growth seemed boundless. But as organizations continue to flatten and world competition intensifies, the smell of burning brakes wafts up to the executive suite. Skidding to a stop, the wheels of vertical advancement have virtually ceased. The thousands of career ladders built and supported between the 1950s and the 1980s are toppling. There is no longer the need, pageantry, or wealth to sustain them.

Seeing the Freedom

A global marketplace and flattening workplaces mean that companies are laying off, deploying, demoting, and retiring workers early. The new playing field is chaotic and complex; it forces some workers into unwelcome expanded roles and others into positions where they "have a job" but are feeling "deskilled." Others, though, are "seeing the freedom." That is, they are *choosing* new roles and new ways of working. Paul, for example, a client who is a marketing director with a food products manufacturer, saw the staff whittled to a bare minimum. He had to redefine his role as a staff consultant, becoming once again a valued player in an evolving organization. He took the initiative to analyze the market and reassess his skills. He rearranged how he used his skills so that they matched what he wanted to do *and* met the needs of division managers and customers. Another client, Laura, an accountant, was initially laid off because the real estate firm where she worked was gobbled up by a larger firm. As she mourned her loss, she also recognized an opportunity for herself as a result of the buyout. Laura negotiated an interim accounting position by convincing her employers that she could ensure a smoother transition. At the same time, she explored other options and planned her future. Ultimately, she decided to start her own accounting service for small businesses; her first client was her former employer. In the past, employers would have avoided such arrangements with ex-workers.

Paul and Laura both realized "it's not the organization as usual." They each looked at what they needed to do to change. Another type of playing field exists: one with fewer bosses, one that is hungry for new ideas and solutions, and one in which, by knowing yourself and seeing opportunity, you can *reapply* for a new job or even invent one. Today the market is much more willing—even eager—to do business with a new or a small firm. Opportunities for independent contractors are far greater in the 1990s than they were in the 1980s.

X

**I've created my own positions, jobs, and myself.
"Preparation" for me was the key . . . my ability to research,
focus, initiate, plan, and communicate, orally and in writing. I
went from working as a seventh-grade teacher to being a
director of fundraising. It took three years of "preparation."**

*—Catharine Cook, director of development,
Center for Applied Special Technology*

Doing the Work

As a result of restructuring, more managers, directors, and vice-presidents are *doing the work*, not delegating it. Line and staff workers are learning to make their own decisions, which influence how the work gets done and what quality of service is provided to customers and clients. In the past, for example, when you visited the dentist, the receptionist greeted you and scheduled appointments and the hygienist checked and cleaned your teeth. Today, in contrast, at the end of your appointment the hygienist pulls out an appointment book and schedules your next visit. The hygienist is running a business within a business. The dental office itself is flatter. It has fewer receptionists, and specialized practitioners are learning to become efficient business managers.

As a specialized practitioner or service provider, you can also use the lattice concept as a valuable communication tool. You might try what Jan Nickerson, managing director of the Prosperity Collaborative, calls a "language" lattice. In your work setting, for example, you might want to convey to your boss that a lack of spirit permeates the company. But the word *spirit* could be misunderstood by your boss and others. Try looking for other words to express your meaning of *spirit*. Build a language lattice. Write the word *spirit*, on a blank piece of paper and jot down all the words that might convey to others what you're trying to say without using the word *spirit*. Use the space freely by writing down any words that come to mind anywhere on the page. Notice the alternatives in the diagram—the lattice—below. Rather than using the word *spirit*, you can now substitute the word *enthusiasm* or one of the other examples and increase the probability that you will be heard.

Language Lattice

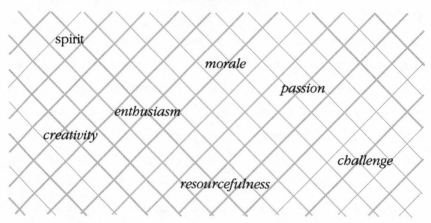

A New Direction

Peter Block, author and consultant, says, "Most of us chose safety when we took the job, and when the open hand of partnership is offered to us, we know there is a price to be paid. The price is uncertainty and anxiety."[3] If "the price is uncertainty and anxiety," the reward is mobility and opportunity. We are all headed in a new direction. Many of my clients know that if they try to stay in one spot for too long or if they hide, they will be devastated by the rapid changes or they will disappear in the quicksand of progress. Most important, they may miss out on fulfilling their own dreams.

Massive organizational, workplace, and marketplace change is a wake-up call for you to follow your own dreams. Today's reality will force you to change, or it will pass you by. Susan, a technical editor, called to schedule a consultation for herself and her husband. "The company I am working for has changed, and the marketplace has done a number on my husband's business," she said. "Our careers seem to be going nowhere. I know what my dream is but have been unable to move it forward, and my husband is frustrated running his business and isn't sure what his dream is. We are afraid, and we need to take control of our careers." "Living your dreams" is one of the best reasons for stretching and redefining the traditional notions of employment to embrace the notion of "self-employment."

Living Your Dream: A Career That Is True to Yourself

Susan's priority was to spend more time with her children, and her professional goal was to find a position similar to the one she had, with one exception: The new position would be with an organization in which she could have a flexible work schedule. To her surprise, Susan advanced on the traditional career ladder. Through a diligent networking effort, she found a position as technical editor and manager of custom publishing with a smaller publishing firm. Now, with a more flexible schedule, she is able to spend part of her time working from home, and when she does attend meetings at the office, they are usually at a time when her children are in school. The price? She earns less money. But she is living her dream.

Susan's husband, Dean, the owner of a small insurance brokerage, took another path. He stepped off the traditional career ladder and onto the career lattice. This meant facing the void of transition. Dean was unsure about what he wanted to do next. "I see myself as someone with a huge amount of energy," he said. "For years I've been focused on building my practice and solving customer problems. Now I feel confused and skeptical. What I've been doing is narrow; I don't feel creative. Besides, my market niche is being taken over by bigger companies. Even though I've made a good living, the business isn't meaningful enough to me to go up against the competition. I'd rather put my energy into figuring out what's next."

Initially, Dean had many questions and few answers. He asked, "Why am I so bored?" "Will finding something else take very long?" and "How will I know when I've found something that is right for me?" These questions exemplify many such questions raised by people who are in career transition. They are healthy and necessary questions. Each represents a piece of a larger puzzle, a minigoal. When all the pieces of the puzzle are in place, achieving the dream is possible. During my sessions with clients, I assure them that, with patience and persistence during this process, together we will answer their questions. Toward the end of a typical session, I give clients one of their questions back to them to answer. This gives them a goal during their transition. Dean asked, for example, "Why am I so bored?" I asked Dean to make a list of the things that were uninteresting to him at work and to share his list with me the next time we met.

During a three-month period, Dean explored his interests, accomplishments, values, and skills. As a result, he closed his business and decided to pursue a sales or sales management position in the insurance industry. Soon Dean received four job offers. Each company knew about Dean's track record but did not know him. Dean, though gratified to receive the offers, chose to turn them down. "At this point," Dean commented, "I've come too far. I must be true to myself; the insurance business, working in a large company, is not me." This experience helped Dean to answer one of his questions, "Is it running my own business that I've grown to dislike, or is it the insurance business?"

Adult career learning leads to understanding your own wisdom and to acquiring the courage to live with and move beyond the doubts.

Competing up the career ladder, stacking one professional job of a similar type onto another, wasn't the answer for Dean. When I asked him to list the things that he most liked doing, he said he enjoyed doing research, making things better, and solving problems. Another of his skills was synthesizing information into a manageable system. Dean boiled down his passions into one phrase: "finding ways to do things differently." This phrase became the catalyst that steered Dean forward.

With Dean's ingenuity, his knowledge of English literature, and his skill in research and problem solving, he secured a part-time job as an assistant librarian. This position might sound farfetched for an insurance broker, but he needed some income and a temporary work situation that felt good to him. This was an opportunity to use some of his skills; more important, with his wife's support and his own determination, he felt less pressure to retreat to the insurance business. Rather than pushing for answers, Dean used the library job to notice what others did for a living and to assess what he wanted and needed.

During this period, Dean discovered that one way he could "do things differently" was to invent marketable goods. He claimed that months before instant coffee bags and bent-handled (back-saver) snow shovels came out on the market, he had thought of these ideas. He had not pursued them because he lacked experience in transforming an idea into a reality. Dean's priority was to focus on what excited him. What he *did* with the idea was less important. The snow shovel was one idea. I proposed that he stay open to other means of "finding ways to do things differently." I said to Dean, "Think back to a time when you owned your own company, when you felt passionate, excited, and energized." "When I doubled my firm size from four to eight people," Dean responded, "and we climbed over the $5 million mark in sales." Then I asked, "What about this experience felt good to you?" "I was creative, a problem solver, and we were expanding. I was leading us forward, not only managing day-to-day operations."

Dean had remembered a past experience in which he felt successful. Up to this point, the experiences he recalled had coagulated into one seemingly cumbersome, uneventful whole, wherein he was unable to delineate his strengths and weaknesses, his needs and passions. To embrace the "self-employed" attitude, we first must untangle and examine our past experiences, as Dean did. We then have a much sharper vision of the road *behind* us, which propels us forward along the road toward a more promising future.

We all have a rich warehouse of knowledge—skills, values, interests, experiences—stored away but accessible. For us to gain access to these hidden treasures, we must deliberately devote time and effort to telling our stories, untangling the past, noticing what excites us, staying open to feedback, evaluating who we are and what we want, and taking the risk of transforming our thoughts and dreams into action.

In helping Dean to expand his vision further, I mentioned the marketplace's need for people to create and develop microniche businesses. These are businesses that provide unique, timely, and valued products or services. For example, Walden Paddlers develops affordable, lightweight kayaks; Executrain designs cutting-edge software training; and Nu-Mega Technologies, Inc., produces specialized software development tools. Knowing about his proven ability and passion for finding ways to do things differently—qualities Dean demonstrated when he formed and expanded his own business—I suggested that Dean look for businesses that were in the expansion stage and might need his talent. Such companies would not be start-ups or established businesses; rather, the best companies for Dean to investigate would be those seeking creative, flexible, and responsible people to help them harness and utilize their resources to develop new systems, products, and services; increase quality; and mentor others toward a common goal.

Dean wondered, "Where do I locate these businesses?" I suggested that he network with associates and colleagues and read trade journals, newspapers, and magazines. First, though, I recommended that Dean do an "I am looking for . . ." summary, an exercise that helps people further refine their goals.

Dean's "I am looking for . . ." summary stated:

I am looking for a small service business that wants to expand. It has grown to a particular level, let's say to $2 million in sales, and it wants to grow to $10 million. I could help them because I am a creative individual who knows how to develop systems, lead people, and sell in a competitive marketplace.

Dean's summary raised an important question to ask his network: "Is there any company you know of that has these characteristics, or is there anyone you know of with whom I could talk to get some suggestions?" As Dean received feedback from his network, he then revised his summary to increase the probability of positive responses.

Take a moment to ask yourself, "What do I really like to do?" and "What do I get excited about?" Try writing down your next step or goal—something that would bring you closer to doing what you really want to do. This exercise is relevant regardless of your work status—unchallenged, laid-off, early-retired or never-want-to-retire, recent college graduate.

Depending on your situation, your goals can span a wide range of possibilities. You could be looking for a mentor, a raise, a promotion, ideas about what school would best suit your educational needs, clarification of your skills and values, a way to communicate more effectively with team members, or a support group to help you develop a business concept.

Dean is well on his way to adopting a "self-employed" attitude. At this time, he has not found a company match, but he feels supported and he is clear about his vision. As he expands his network, he will find a company that is in the expansion stage and matches his skills and passion. And the timing is right: The marketplace is filled with niche businesses that are hungering to expand.

A "Self-Employed" Reality Check

At this point, you may be thinking, "I'm more 'self-employed' than I thought. How can I improve my work life?" You might also be wondering, "Just how 'self-employed' am I?" Both questions are catalysts for continuing to learn about yourself and about this concept. The "self-employed" inventory that follows will help you to answer these questions. It is designed as a source of information and as a guide for your learning.

"Self-Employed" Inventory

Think about these questions and how you typically behave on the job. Then answer "yes" or "no." If you have answered "yes" to most of these questions, you can continue to fine-tune what you do and teach others. If you answered "no" to most of the questions, you have a sense of some of the ways you think and act and of some of the things you need to learn.

—continued

1. Do you believe that your current job is guaranteed or that you will have the same customers forever?

2. Do you go beyond your job description?
   Do you volunteer for projects?
   Do you identify problems?
   Do you initiate solutions?
   Do you look beyond the hours you work to the task or job that needs to be accomplished?

3. Do you seek out others with whom to share ideas and advice?

4. Do you take an inventory of your skills every four to six months?

5. Do you ask your customers—on a regular basis—what you can do to improve your service delivery or product quality?

6. Do you enjoy what you do at least two-thirds of the time?

7. Do you make it a point to learn something new every week?

8. Do you ask questions rather than simply accept what comes your way?

9. Do you develop flexible action plans as you assess your options to change?

10. Do you believe that you are responsible for your career or job?

Write your answers to the questions on a separate piece of paper. Now look at your completed inventory. For question 2, you may have answered yes to "Identify problems" but may have answered no to "Initiate solutions." In one area, identifying problems, you feel confident and have examples to prove your proficiency. On the other hand, initiating solutions is an area in which you've had little practice. Or perhaps you are used to thinking "that's someone else's job." In my work with managers in organizations, I've heard them complain about a lack of worker initiative. In today's complex work environments, managers, owners, or colleagues can't possibly have all the answers. If initiating and presenting new ideas is one of your strengths, there are ample opportunities in the marketplace for you. Try to remember this rule:

Initiate: For every problem you recognize, think of at least two solutions. Then take the risk and present them.

Customers will thank you for thinking things through, and your boss will recognize you as an independent thinker who is able to make a contribution without being asked. It's as natural as sweeping your kitchen floor *before* your spouse asks you! As you read the following chapters, consider your answers to the "self-employed" inventory. Can you incorporate some of what you've learned as a means to turn a "no" into a "yes" or to improve your "self-employed" attitude?

2

FACING THE DRAGON— YOUR WORK FEARS

Replace fear with passion

EMPLOYED ATTITUDE

Dependent Mindset

If I just put my head down and work harder, I'll be safe. I can ignore my fears of knowing myself, losing my job, or understanding my passion.

SELF-EMPLOYED ATTITUDE

Independent and Interdependent Mindset

I will face the dragon—my work fears—and replace fear with passion. I will share my ideas; identify my skills, values, and desires; and ask questions to clarify my focus both for myself and for my company.

THE DRAGON IN ALL OF US—individuals and organizations—is our fear of change. Fear of change holds back our potential, the contributions we could make, and our ability to experience the wonders and adventures of life. I can remember a time in my youth, for example, when I dreamed about living and working in California. I had heard that San Francisco was a delightful city and that Big Sur was a spectacular place. But I was afraid to go. Disturbed and pained by my fear, I sought the counsel of George, a psychotherapist. After I talked for approximately fifteen minutes, George looked straight at me and simply said, "Go." That was all I needed—validation for my passion. His permission gave me permission to cut through my doubts. Shortly after that session, I spent two of the best years of my life living and working in San Francisco. Fear could have held me back.

Traditional self-employment—owning one's own business—is an expression of self. I like to think that those who are traditionally self-employed choose this path, at least in part, as an expression of their passion. In this book, although I'm not advocating that you own your own business, I do support those of you who believe you can do work that resonates with your inner core. Your inner core is organic—a place with no preservatives, a central part of you. It is a place where safety and adventure coexist. Safety is the inner security that comes from knowing yourself; adventure, the ability to risk or to trade the known for the unknown. Safety and adventure coexist when you know yourself well enough to step into—not be forced into—new frontiers. Over time, all the shoulds, oughts, demands, and distractions of life can diminish but not extinguish our passion. In all of us is the ability to live more authentically, closer to our passion.

Permission to Be Your Authentic Self

We Are All Self-Employed gives you "permission" to do your work from your passion and your integrity. The reason to challenge your fears and experience your passion is to do your best work and live a fuller life. "I'm a soft-spoken leader," remarked one executive. "That's my power. Now that I know that, I want to find a place where I can use my being." This chapter will help you overcome your fears by demonstrating specific ways that you can do your work and live your life practically and passionately.

I've survived and succeeded, and I plan to continue to do so in our capitalistic economy. People I talk with casually, as well as my clients, plan to do the same. But like our forebears, who gave up the wilderness and the land, many of us have simply "joined up," clinging to the traditional models of work. As our organizational structures are being reshaped, *we* are being reshaped; our identities are being radically altered. Invisible T-shirts (and in some cases, visible ones) inscribed with IBM, DEC, Kodak, GM, Du Pont, or AT&T are sometimes impossible icons to wash off. In many instances, it takes skill, perseverance, patience, and time—a lot of it—to shed an organizational identity. One of my clients held his stomach as he complained, "I know conceptually that I can no longer be loyal to my company in the same way, but I don't *feel* that way. I'll sue the company if they try to let me go." He was really saying, "I'm scared. I grew up in the company during the past thirty years. What would I do? Who would I be without it?"

Face to Face with the Dragon

Realize you're not alone. Corporate goliaths and smaller entities— small- to medium-size companies—are trying to survive and compete. As many of you are learning and struggling not only to survive but also to go beyond survival, your expertise will be useful only for as long as you are benefiting an organization and its customers. I can remember a time not too long ago when a forty-three-year-old manager said, "If I could only get into Digital, I could stay there until my retirement." Organizations, whether they employ 100,000 or 10 workers, are no longer—and I doubt they ever were—safe harbors. They are, though, important places where people *can* make a contribution and earn a livelihood.

Challenge the dragon! To succeed, not simply survive, we must change. The process is not necessarily easy, but we do it incrementally, practically, and creatively, with a spirit for adventure. The alternative— living in fear—is decidedly no way to work or live.

On the following page, I compare what it takes "to live fearfully" with what it takes "to live passionately." This comparison is important so that you can make choices between the two. The list of values on page 54 then shows what it takes to overcome any fears and how better to express your passion. Among the points listed, I'm partial to the phrase "*courage*, to pursue what works for you." Helping individuals summon and use their courage to pursue what works for them is at the core of my consulting practice. If you do not learn this point, you will undoubtedly feel unhappy, uncommitted, depressed, or on edge. One of the worst feelings I've experienced occurs when I undergo a prolonged period of being unhappy with my work. At such times, who I am is disconnected from my work; I watch the clock and ache inside; unchallenged, I feel that my life is passing me by. I am dedicated to helping others work through and overcome similar experiences. Confronting yourself and giving birth to your joy do take courage. If you have read this far, then courage and freedom are well within your grasp.

You Can Choose How You Live

Compare the two lists below. On a piece of paper write down the items that best describe you and your way of life.

To Live Fearfully	*To Live Passionately*
I react to and move from one thing to the next.	I defer gratification.
I stay closed to feedback.	I engage in continuous learning.
I do only what others say.	I pursue what works for me.
I ignore what I am thinking and feeling.	I listen to my own internal messages.
I often retreat into a shell.	I am able to say, "This is who I am."
I resist support.	I can ask for support.
I'm often blind to the value of my dreams.	I can see all or part of my dream.
I give up too soon.	I persevere when things seem least hopeful.

What It Takes to Express Your Passion

- **Patience**, to defer gratification
- **Self-permission**, to engage in continuous learning
- **Courage**, to pursue what works for you
- **Openness**, to hear feedback from others and to listen to your own internal messages
- **Boldness**, to say, "This is who I am."
- **Humility**, to ask for support
- **Vision**, to see all or part of your dream
- **Tenacity**, to persevere when things seem least hopeful

Suspending Fear: Passion in Process

Walter, a marketing manager with a communications company, was dreading a performance appraisal meeting with his boss. The organization had been downsizing for the past two years; colleagues in Walter's division and in others had been laid off. Several projects Walter had been working on for the past six months had not succeeded, thus adding to his anxiety. Unlike in the past, there were more fits and starts and fewer results to report. Walter, speculating that he would hear "bad news" at the meeting, sought my services to discuss his anxiety and to explore what he could do that would be supportive to himself and the company.

Rather than advising Walter to wait for the boom to drop, I asked him if he would try suspending his speculations. He agreed, and I followed with, "If you didn't have fear, what would you do in this situation?" After some thoughtful moments, he answered, "I'd not only listen to what my boss had to say, but I would tell my boss what was on my mind. I'd tell him about the changes that I saw in my job and in the organization."

Like many of us, Walter had learned *not* to question the boss. "Don't question, ask"—this message has been drilled into and is deeply embedded in our psyches. Our parents, teachers, coaches, and managers—all bosses—say in one way or another, "I'm in control," "I know better," or simply, "Do what you're told—because I said so." These messages teach us to second-guess ourselves. They inhibit our creativity and spontaneity, our spirit for adventure. We learn to follow rather than to participate, invent, and contribute.

Fortunately, it seems that, slowly and painfully, the tides are shifting. Companies are learning that they *need* people who question and contribute—those who understand their own needs and the business's goals, see what needs to be done today and in the longer term, and are prepared to participate in change. As their structures flatten, companies are collaborating more with workers. Problem solving increasingly requires specific expertise, as intensified competition calls for effective and efficient team participation. Workers like Walter are getting the message that it is their responsibility to take an active role in their own development and that of the company.

Walter took control by stepping back to analyze what he *had* been doing and under what kinds of conditions. After reviewing his project requirements, he realized that his job basically involved researching and planning project feasibility, not managing people, in a work environment that was trying to stabilize. He saw that he was no longer acting as a marketing manager, a role perhaps better suited to a growing environment. Clarifying his current role and seeing it within the context of a changed corporate environment became a crucial catalyst for establishing what he called a "conversational approach," as opposed to a subordinate one, for the meeting he had feared.

As Walter talked about what he actually *did*, he learned what his job really entailed. Many of my clients don't know what they do—they just "do." To represent themselves or navigate unfamiliar territory, they must find the words that describe what they do and create a bridge toward choice and positive change. With this insight, Walter brought his own agenda to the meeting. He asked questions, made comments, and shared solutions, but he did *not* try to control his boss's behavior or predict what the outcomes might be.

One of the things we can ask ourselves in our workplaces is...

If I didn't have fear, what would I do within my job or career?

Find a quiet spot, and for a couple of minutes give this question some thought. Write down on a piece of paper the first thing that comes to your mind. Writing your fear down is a way to get it out of you and face it. Seeing your fear is the first step to moving beyond it. Remember my experience with George? Now, write down one action step that you might take to overcome your fear.

Fear constricts and binds you; it keeps you from risking new ways of solving your problems and so gives rise to still more self-defeating behavior. Fear, incidentally, is always fear of some future thing. I have observed that as soon as a person confronts or challenges whatever he is afraid of, the fear vanishes.

—*Virginia Satir,* Peoplemaking

One of Walter's fears was that his boss would not listen to him if Walter shared what was on his mind. An action step he took was to prioritize and write out his agenda so that he could present his thoughts succinctly.

Walter's Agenda

1. *To talk about what he had accomplished within the context of a changed organization.*

   Walter's recent accomplishments, although different from those in the past, were aligned with present organizational needs. Through his foresight, his flexibility, and his ability to analyze the current situation, Walter had created a different yet necessary role.

2. *To share what he and others were feeling about the organization.*

   Walter had noticed the dissatisfaction and struggles of his colleagues. They, as he had been, were reluctant to talk about their despair. Rather than letting fear dominate, Walter shared some of his feelings and those of his co-workers. His boss listened, for he too had feelings about the changes in the company.

3. *To ask specifically what the current goals of the division and the organization were.*

   Walter began to see that it was his responsibility to seek out information. With information, he could make choices and influence others. Without it, he had much less control.

4. *To continue making a contribution.*

   Using the information he received from his boss, Walter made specific suggestions about how he could continue to contribute.

His boss listened. Walter's performance appraisal meeting turned into a constructive conversation and a gateway for future collaboration with his boss. Walter is still working as a marketing manager with the same communications company, but Walter is not the same. He has learned that by confronting his fear, by changing the way he thinks about a situation, and by taking action he can make a difference in his own life and make a contribution to the organization.

Ultimately, no matter where I am, I determine what needs to be done and how to do it. I've worked as a laborer and an executive, and there was little difference in how I approached my work in both of those positions. Even in positions where you are told to do what you are supposed to do, there is freedom in determining how the work is done. The "how" for me is internal as well as what is visible to others.

—Pierrette Kelly, president, Mainstay Enterprises

Below you'll see the benefits of expressing your passion. One benefit is that you'll feel a greater inner sense of security and express it outwardly. This aspect is a joy. Believe it or not, you can earn less money and feel more secure. The security comes from feeling that you are doing work that is part of—not apart from—you. How can anyone take that from you? It's yours.

Benefits of Expressing Your Passion

You will . . .

- feel better—more energetic, more whole.
- attract people with similar values.
- experience a GOOD tired feeling at the end of the day.
- find a job or a project that fits with your goals and skills.
- feel a greater inner sense of security and express it outwardly.
- make a unique contribution to the world.

◪

**All self-actualized people have a cause they believe in, a
vocation they are devoted to. [They] seem to do what they do for
the sake of ultimate, final values, which is for the sake of
principles which seem *intrinsically worthwhile* [author's
emphasis]. They protect and love these values,
and if the values are threatened, they will be aroused to
indignation, action, and often self-sacrifice.**

—*A. H. Maslow,* The Farther Reaches of Human Nature

An Agenda for Unchallenged Workers

Unchallenged workers can borrow from Walter's agenda to create
opportunity for themselves and their organization. If you are unchallenged, your agenda could look like this:

Agenda for Developing a "Self-Employed" Attitude

1. *Inventory your skills and accomplishments every six months.*
   Write down specific examples that illustrate your skills and
   accomplishments.

2. *Seek out information about company/division goals.*
   Network with colleagues and workers in other divisions. Find out
   if new products and services are being planned. There may be an
   opportunity for you.

3. *Discover ways to make a contribution.*
   Match your skills and accomplishments with company/division goals.

4. *Share your plans and feelings with your colleagues and manager.*
   Find support for and get feedback on your ideas. Ask others for
   their help to clarify and align your desires with company/divi-
   sion goals.

Your Present Situation

Don Quixote, Cervantes's courageous hero, charged the windmills, which were symbols of change. His advances were thwarted by progress, the windmill's arms. The windmills of today—advanced technology, the end of the cold war, global competition—are impossible to defy. Despite gallant efforts—individual or organizational—fighting to maintain the old ways or holding on to the status quo, you will eventually be blown over by the windmills' powerful force.

The reality—"we are all self-employed"—means taking responsibility for your job productivity and career mobility and for serving others. Thinking "My job is safe. I doubt I would ever lose it" is a defiant belief. The same is true for any organization that continues to institute a "no-layoff" policy. Companies must do all they can to ensure their survival, restructuring as change necessitates. To believe otherwise is to succumb to the dragon—the fear of change.

Quixotic heroics may very well feed your fantasies, but to challenge the dragon within and outside yourself, first understand your present work situation. The following exercise will help you to challenge the dragon—confront your fears regarding change—by writing down how you and your job *have* changed. This is a bold step toward seeing your abilities and making other changes.

The purpose of the exercise is to help you see your current work situation, how it has changed, and how you have changed. Seeing your current actions listed in the "Now" column and comparing them with your former activities, listed in the "Then" column, will give you information to assess your progress and to make future plans. You may learn, for example, that you have made more changes than you thought. On reflection, you may feel especially good about your present ability to

⁜

You and Your Job: Then and Now

More likely than not, during the past six months or even less, you and your job have changed. Here are two examples: (1) You had been taking orders from your boss, whereas now you are contributing ideas to a team that includes your boss, and (2) You had been managing people, whereas now you are managing projects. Other examples are shown on the chart below.

Then	*Now*
I basically did what my boss asked.	I collaborate more with a team.
I managed twenty people.	I manage projects, not people.
I worked at the company office.	I work two days a week from home.
My accounts were scattered through the Northwest.	I'm focused on the New York City market.
Professional education was not a priority.	I'm constantly reading professional journals and books.

On a separate piece of paper, draw a similar chart. Label one column "Then" and the other "Now." Think of ways in which you and your job have changed. Be specific. In the "Then" column, write down one of the characteristics of your past. Opposite each "Then" response, in the "Now" column, give an example of the way you or your job situation is now.

---

collaborate with a team. Now that you are more conscious of this change, ask yourself, "What skills have I developed? Which do I want to develop further?" Is one of your skills your ability to negotiate with other team members?

Replacing Fear with Passion

Joanne, a planning manager with a *Fortune* 100 company, felt stymied in her job. She had a prestigious title, she was earning plenty of money, her boss considered her a valued expert, and she had earned the respect of her colleagues as the first woman in the company to have attained such a position.

Although she appeared successful to others, Joanne had grown tired of planning and wanted to move into a leadership role where she could use her creative talents. But she felt conflicted because she was afraid to give up her status and income. She liked her colleagues and believed the company she had been with for the past five years was on the verge of becoming a recognized leader in the industry. Joanne asked, "How can I move on in my career to where I feel passionate about my work, remain visible, and also earn a good living?" Joanne's intent was not to leave but to help lead the company through an organizational restructuring process. To "let go," she found it helpful to see herself as self-employed—to see that only she could be responsible for her career mobility. Even though her boss recognized her as a valued expert, from his point of view she was a valued expert in the "right" position.

Joanne needed to challenge the dragon. She was a superb problem solver and initiator of solutions, but rather than continuing to plan and do, she needed to step back and take an inventory of her skills, values, and interests and to assess how she might apply them in the company. As a result, she identified two skills that she wanted to market and felt passionate about: leading and communicating. Leading involved seeing and articulating how the culture needed to change, and communicating included her ability to influence, negotiate, and build a team around a common goal. Her inventory gave her plenty of marketing material, but she still needed to confront her fears. She isolated two: (1) reprisal from her boss if she were to move and (2) her own reservations about her ability to take on a leadership role.

Joanne talked about her fears as a means of airing and resolving her feelings. Regardless of *your* level, compensation, or professional expertise, it is crucial to your mobility to talk about your feelings. Often this process is overlooked or consciously denigrated as "soft stuff." What *looks* "soft," however, may be the hardest obstacle to overcome. Joanne went on to formulate a plan for building a bridge between her current situation and her future goals. At a company meeting, she caught wind of an opportunity whereby she could potentially help Laurel, a vice-president, to streamline her division. Joanne met with Laurel to share her knowledge about some of the problems Laurel was facing and to propose how she herself, in a leadership role, could help the vice-president to plan, communicate, and implement change. Joanne accepted Laurel's offer to take on a part-time leadership role.

The other part of Joanne's plan was to view the shift toward leadership as half of her job. She remained active as planning manager, at least for a while, as she tested her new role. She is now making program contributions to another division, programs that could be adopted as models for change for the whole company. She is gaining marketable experience, developing visibility in another part of the company, and feeling more passionate about her work. She has a parachute, or fallback position—a continuing relationship with her former boss and colleagues—should things not work out as expected. And she realizes that not even this parachute comes with a guarantee. Joanne discovered that letting go of her past and moving toward her passion took courage and ingenuity. None of us can or should make a career move by taking one quantum leap. Developing a "self-employed" attitude—overcoming your fears and living your passion—is an incremental process.

There Is a Price for Ignoring Your Passion

The price for remaining stuck in an unrewarding job is a gnawing, tired, angry feeling of unfulfillment, a sense that you could be *doing* more with your life and that you could be *feeling* better about what you do and how you contribute to others. Doing what you really want to do, even partially, isn't easy. I've witnessed numerous individuals who give up at the halfway point or do not try at all. They choose to hear, "Getting a job is tough," "Finding another position in the company is nearly impossible," or "Why speak your mind? The company doesn't care." People buy into the majority voice before exploring alternatives. They bury their passion under yet another layer of fear or skepticism and do only what is practical: charging obediently, blindly, against that fire-breathing dragon.

Don Juan teaches Carlos Castaneda about the notion "we are all self-employed" in *The Fire from Within*:

> *To have a path of knowledge, a path with a heart, makes for a joyful journey . . . and is the only conceivable way to live. We must then think carefully about our paths before we set out on them, for by the time a person discovers that his path "has no heart," the path is ready to kill him. At that point few of us have the courage to abandon the path, lethal as it may be, because we have invested so much in it, and to choose a new path seems so dangerous, even irresponsible. And so we continue dutifully, if joylessly, along.*[1]

Lunch with a Colleague

From my perspective, writing a book is a collaborative journey: My colleagues and friends give support and contribute ideas, and I gather and synthesize information and put the words on paper (computer!).

Over the years, I have made an effort to invite people who have been helpful to join me for a thank-you breakfast or lunch. Inevitably, our conversations focus partially on our personal careers.

I hadn't seen Luca, an art director, in almost a year, although we had had several telephone conversations. While I was writing this book, Luca reviewed a draft of the manuscript and made several useful and heartfelt comments. When we sat down to lunch, I was startled by Luca's lack of eye contact. For the first ten minutes of our meeting, he sat hunched over, looking down at his plate and asking me questions about my life. I was puzzled and asked, "So what's going on for you?" Luca's eyes met mine. He paused, then said, "I'm feeling confused, lost. I'm stuck in the same place, working part-time. I don't seem to be getting anywhere with my career."

Luca is a fifty-five-year-old man who grew up in a small town, became successful in advertising and public relations, got knocked off the ladder, and is now on his own—self-employed. Luca has pride and, like many people I've met, is afraid of stumbling and bumbling in the marketplace. "I've paid my dues," Luca reminded me—a common proclamation. He continued: "I wish I had learned at twenty-three what Paola, my daughter, already knows about herself and her career." "What does Paola know?" I asked. Luca began a verbal list: "She takes risks, trusts her intuition, believes change is good and it's OK to make mistakes. She champions herself and doesn't wait for others' opinions before she takes action."

I thought that was quite a list, and said, "I know what you mean. I wish I'd known those things when *I* was twenty-three." Luca responded, "Another thing: I doubt she has this list written down anywhere, and I'm not sure how conscious she is of her attributes. She doesn't have a mentor; she just lives in these ways. Sometimes it's hard to believe we both live in the same world. Paola isn't afraid to make things happen."

As Luca talked, I looked at him, thinking to myself that Paola did have a mentor, and that if more people became conscious of and *wrote down* constructive behaviors for overcoming their fears, they would learn to trust their intuition: Their list would become part of their plan for acting on their intuition. "Luca," I said, "Paola's words are a template for change. They give her inspiration and courage." "Her words are a *golden* template," Luca added. "I need to learn from her. It's time I stop hiding behind my plans and start meeting more people. I need to tell them what I can do for them." "Luca, I want to remind you," I said, "Paola has had a mentor . . . you." Luca's eyes opened wide and he smiled.

Before we parted, Luca wrote down his "golden template" and handed it to me.

Luca's Golden Template

I will . . .

- talk about my feelings.
- risk sharing my ideas with others.
- plan, then test my plan. I won't just plan, plan, plan.
- meet with friends more often for support.
- champion myself, as Paola does; I won't wait to hear others' opinions before I take action.
- view mistakes as stepping-stones.

You may want to write your own golden template. Think of two or three guiding principles—messages that you could consistently give yourself to grow and progress in your work and your life.

Patience Is an Active Process

We have explored the fear of change and seen the importance of knowing the current realities of the workplace. Before we go further, I want to address "impatience" as an obstacle to your passion, job productivity, and career mobility. Unfortunately, in our society—organizations, schools, families—we get little support for the rediscovery process. Messages like "Getting there shouldn't be such a struggle" abound and feed our impatience. The resulting "shoulds" block our rediscovery—our passion, productivity, and mobility. Statements like, "I'm too old for this; I should know where I'm going by now" or "I should do what others think is best" inhibit our progress. They bury our inner voice, our true needs and wants.

Believing "we are all self-employed" requires that we make an active cognitive shift from "I should" to "I need" or "I want." These needs or wants are available to us when we pause and learn to be patient, primarily with ourselves. "I'm forty-three years old and I'm burning out," complained Ron, a successful entrepreneur. "I've developed this pattern of going from one thing to the next. My career is important to me, but I can't go on this way." Ron believed that he *should* always be doing things. Exhausted by this pattern, he no longer enjoyed running his business. After we talked at length about the pattern, I asked him if he could learn to be patient with himself as he tried some new ways of coping with change and reestablishing his career. He seemed relieved—he needed permission from someone else to readjust his pace and to take a look at what was no longer working in his life.

Over several months, Ron discovered that being patient was an active learning process that involved making daily decisions. It was important for him not to charge into another business—a box—for

doing so would put him back into his familiar yet debilitating and fre-
netic pattern. Rather, with patience, Ron learned to name his feelings,
talk about the skills and values that were most important to him, and
experiment with how he might get his needs and wants met by working part-time.

*I often say to my clients, "Slow it up." Many are relieved to receive
permission to try another way.*

Patience Can Lead to Passion

The list below suggests some ways that you can be patient as a means
toward living your passion.

What to Do

- Share your ideas, but hold off and think carefully before committing to
  action.
- Be curious and gather facts.
- Share your honest, intuitive opinion.
- Do things step by step and follow through.
- Confront problems and trust that you'll find solutions.
- Tell others you haven't made a decision yet, but you *will* get back to
  them.
- Do part-time work as you search for what you really want.
- Work for the common good.

Regarding the last point of this list, "Work for the common good,"
finding your path—the work you want to do—means that you'll
inevitably work for the good of others. Ruth, a public relations specialist,
has found an expression for her passion: influencing others. She is dedicated to serving her clients in the software industry, helping them

to deliver their unique messages through the media and to run profitable businesses. She is giving them her communications expertise and her passion. In turn, they are providing tools that help their customers do their work more effectively.

Stepping beyond Fear: Caring and Respecting

"In meetings," began Martha, an administrator, "I'm usually the one who makes sense of and exposes what the real issues are. It's as though I'm a voice for others." In a consultation with Martha, I asked her, "How do you know that you are expressing what others are thinking?" "People sit up and their eyes open wide," she replied. "Often after a meeting, there are those who say, 'You spoke for many of us.' " As she told her story, she glowed but quickly dismissed her talent as nothing special. I've talked with several professionals like Martha, who make statements and tell stories about their talents. They say, "I can see the bigger picture and describe what I see to others," "As a manager, I bring out people's best talents, and as a result they feel good about their work and become more productive," or "I enjoy and am challenged by shifting into different roles." They proceed to back up their statements with stories. But as Martha had done, they pass off their talent by saying, "Big deal."

In these situations, I am quick to say, "Take care of and respect what seems to be natural to you. Passion comes in many forms, some not as obvious as others. You can take care of and respect your abilities by suspending your judgment and practicing curiosity and observation. Notice other people's eyes and posture, and become aware of what they say. They are telling you about you."

Another way to respect and care for your talent is to keep a journal. Write down specifically what you did and how you felt in the process. On a sales call, for example, do you listen to the client? Do clients then consistently respond by buying your product or service, or do they refer others to you? If you have already written about this scenario several times in your journal, most likely you have a talent or a skill that you've honed: listening. Don't ignore your talent, even though it may seem obvious to you; take care of and respect it. Document your specific behavior; note how you use your listening skills. Do you paraphrase what the client has said? Do you share some of your own experiences that might mirror the client's? Is your eye contact direct and sincere? These are the skills that have made you a successful salesperson. Take care of and respect them as you call on clients. Share them as you step toward a "self-employed" attitude and look toward enhancing your career.

3

INTEGRATING INDEPENDENCE AND INTERDEPENDENCE

Be yourself and collaborate with others

EMPLOYED ATTITUDE

Dependent Mindset

I am dependent on the company and customers. They know what I do best and what is best for me. They will take care of me.

SELF-EMPLOYED ATTITUDE

Independent and Interdependent Mindset

I will integrate independence and interdependence. I will strive to be myself and collaborate with others.

T HE TRANSITION FROM SUMMER TO FALL is ushered in by warm days and cool nights, turning leaves, and crisp apples. It is fall as I write this, and each autumn I pay special attention to another sign of seasonal change: the flocks of wild geese migrating south, whose majesty inspires a sense of wonder and joy. They also symbolize the bridge between independence and interdependence, the subject of this chapter.

Every one of these birds is *independent*, distinctly airborne, propelled by its own power. Each is also *interdependent*, taking cues from one another and flying in exquisite formation. They seem free, yet purposeful. They are organized, yet unrestricted as they fly toward a common goal.

The geese fly for days, tirelessly, rotating positions, each taking a turn at the helm. They share the leadership responsibility so that burnout is rare, and if one does falter, two others move forward to support the one in trouble. Imagine if individuals and organizations learned to function this way!

Dependent on the System

This chapter is for those of you who feel shackled by the constraints of dependence on an organization and are looking for the support to "be yourself," doing your best work, *and* to collaborate with others. Many of the individuals whom I coach and counsel appear successful from an outsider's point of view. They have things, titles, and power. But paradoxically, they are dependent, driven by and beholden to a system. The system is composed of their clients, customers, parents, family, spouse, organization, *and* themselves. "My problem," lamented Robert, a chief investment officer, "is that I'm about to become a partner in the firm, but I'm not sure I want the position. Fifteen years ago, I sort of fell into what I'm doing, and I've been successful, although my success has not really been by design." We are all part of the system in varying degrees. This is not a judgment, good or bad, but a practical observation designed to free and inspire you. Many of you wonder, "Have my choices been of my design?" and others ask, "What is in my control and how do I go about taking control?"

Together we are all going through life alone.
—Lily Tomlin

Dependence Is Not Support

Dependence is *not* support; the two are different. Support is the direction that mentors give their protégés. It is also part of the synergy athletes must have to form an exceptional team or that world leaders must utilize to create peace. Without support, individuals and teams could not function effectively, and our world would probably be uninhabitable. Support is a vital form of sustenance and can be the underpinning for growth and change. Several years ago, after nineteen years of marriage, Greg, a good friend of mine, went through a divorce. For about six months, we had coffee together once a week; I never said much, but he knew I cared. To this day, Greg reminds me that my sitting with him, or, in his words, "just being there," pulled him through a devastating time.

Support in its most positive light teaches people to be their best, most authentic selves in their work. There is something pure about support. Dependence, on the other hand, teaches people to suppress who they are—to sublimate their passion, resist their creativity, and compromise their values. As the job market fluctuates and corporations restructure, many professionals today feel *more* dependent as a result. People believe it when they hear, "You'd be *lucky* to find another job." Or they capitulate, thinking, "Why should I even ask or look? There just aren't any jobs." Or they adopt, consciously or unconsciously, a dispassionate attitude: "I have no power; I'll keep my head down and hope for the best."

Dependence is also rooted in another extreme, what Sarah, a systems manager, referred to as the "golden handcuffs." She explained, "That's when the company paid me so much that I couldn't afford to leave. Out of one side of my boss's mouth, he told me I was doing a good job and reminded me I was earning in the six figures. But I was not allowed to attend the organization's strategy meetings. It was killing me to compromise my values; I didn't have decision-making power. Finally, to the disbelief of my boss, my colleagues, my parents, and my friends, I left."

I clung to my business mother for twenty-six years.
I valued myself because of who IBM thought I was.

—Albert, a former project team leader at IBM

Dependence Is as Impure as Support Can Be Pure

Dependence is our responsibility. Those who accept it and choose to remain dependent live by the creed "As long as they pay me and I get my benefits, I'll do what they want." Some people live by another creed, equally grounded in dependence: "I'll manipulate the system to get what I want." Christyn, a corporate systems executive, was on maternity leave. Her yearly compensation package included a substantial bonus, whose amount was based on individual and organizational performance criteria. After three months at home with her newborn, Christyn decided not to return to work. It was September and she expected her bonus the following January. Christyn called her boss and asked, "If I decide not to come back to work, could you still pay me my annual bonus?" Her boss retorted, "Over my dead body! If you want to return to work for the rest of the year, *then* you might be eligible for your full bonus." Traditionally self-employed people get paid for what they do—their performance. This is how they earn their living. Christyn found out "we are all self-employed." Her dependent, manipulative request went unrewarded.

Dependence is . . .

- ≣ feeling constrained, as though you are living someone else's life.
- ≣ working in a profession that someone else chose for you; fear and obligation are the reasons that you continue.
- ≣ staying closed to feedback about yourself and changes in the world.

Independence

Independence—your freedom—is a lifelong, evolutionary—at times, revolutionary—process that requires courage, patience, awareness, wisdom, and the ability to compete. In the United States and in other parts of the world, we have "constitutional" independence, a legal right. But "live" independence—actively pursuing your dreams and serving others—is a different story. One does not automatically guarantee the other. My grandfather came here because he had heard this was a free land. He lived his freedom—persevering, innovating, and producing—independent of contradictory opinions. While many of his peers had a position—climbed the ladder—he didn't have words for the way that he worked. He made choices; he "burned the grass."

Our ancestors earned their independence, but their legacy has been lost over the years. Sometimes our independence seems elusive as we battle the dragon, our thoughtless activity, and our unexamined priorities. We believe that independence is reserved for the elite. We seek and wait for approval before we make a suggestion or decision, invent something new, or follow our dreams. During a twelve-year period, Scott, an office equipment salesman, fell unwittingly into a web of dependence that included repeat clients, financial rewards, and career advancement. To an outsider, Scott's situation might have looked pretty good, and for a time it was. With another promotion in the offing, he questioned, "Is this my destiny? My colleagues think this offer is a great opportunity, but I feel I need a change." As his consultant, I guided Scott through a process of intensive personal searching. "Intensive personal searching" represents Scott's independence: the need to step back and make conscious choices, by design, and live with them.

Independence is . . .

- ▤ knowing yourself and continuing your journey of self-discovery.
- ▤ choosing work that benefits you *and* others.
- ▤ feeling the freedom to change and changing when you have grown beyond what you have been doing.

If We Take Care of Them—

Do Our Job—They Will Take Care of Us

Too many of us have bought into the myth "If we take care of them—do our job—they will take care of us." Another rendition of this myth would be "They are my employers; I work *for* them. If I am loyal [in other words, dependent], they will be loyal to me [guarantee me a job]." People behave as if this code were etched into the side of an anchor. When the anchor is tossed into rough seas, talented but dependent people go overboard. Experiencing and developing new beliefs will greatly enhance your chances for success and survival. One belief is that "no etching is permanent." Marianne, a biotech documentation specialist, *believed*, "I have to kill myself to make a decent living." She was working seventy-five hours per week. In her first consultation with me, she wondered, "Do I have the right skills for the job?" After listening to her stories about her successes, I determined that she had ample skills. I explained to Marianne, "Our skills alone do not determine our direction, feelings of success, and personal and professional development. They take a backseat to our beliefs, the rudder that steers our direction and quality of life." I asked Marianne, "What do you want to be different in your work, your life?" She answered, "One thing is to work not more then forty-five hours per week." Currently, Marianne is examining her old beliefs, the ones that are no longer working. In addition, she is redefining her job and how she does it. These are steps toward adopting a new belief that she *can* work forty-five hours per week, earn an income between $75,000 and $100,000, and have meaningful work. Following is a list of other typical beliefs and myths that are held by people in career transition and may curb independent efforts.

You Can Change Your Beliefs

Changing how you think is an essential part of the process of self-understanding. Your beliefs could be holding you back.

1. *Myth:* If I change, I may fail.
    Empowered: Change is a natural part of living life.

2. *Myth:* Someone else will have the answer for me.
    Empowered: There is great joy in discovery; I can find or create the answer.

3. *Myth:* What my parents, spouse, and friends think is more important than what I think.
    Empowered: I will consider what others think as I formulate my own thoughts.

4. *Myth:* I'm too old [or too young] to change.
    Empowered: I can change at any age.

5. *Myth:* Other people get what they want, not me.
    Empowered: Understanding and articulating what I want is a key to achieving my goals.

6. *Myth:* My work should satisfy all my needs.
    Empowered: Balance is most important in my life; satisfying work is part of that balance.

7. *Myth:* I shouldn't ask.
    Empowered: When I ask, I learn.

"Don't Swim with a Full Stomach"

How many times did your mother say, "Don't swim with a full stomach"? How many of you went swimming anyway? If you did, was the lifeguard called? Did you get cramps? Few if any of you would answer "yes" to either question. If we don't try new things and ignore the "wisdom" of others, we will never know our own reality.

In the work world, it is as if too many workers have full stomachs and are afraid to swim. They continue to behave in detrimental, non-productive ways because of their attachment to past successes or to what someone told them years ago, or even yesterday. When people are dependent on another individual's thoughts or on groupthink, they eventually become afraid, lose hope, or never take a risk. Cindy, who had received her company's top design award, stopped taking risks. She lived with the message "You've made it to the top. Why take a risk? You might get cramps." Pamela, a public relations executive, had worked diligently for years to achieve her position and contribute to the company. She was also being sexually harassed by her new boss. For months, despite her anguish, she lived with the myth "You've got a great job [your stomach is full]; you should be thankful." Eventually, she found support and challenged the myth, "You have a great job; ignore your boss's harassment": She confronted her boss, hired a lawyer, and won a lawsuit against her boss.

Interdependence

Whether you work in or outside of an organization, one-half of being self-employed is *in*dependence and the other half is *inter*dependence. They both take work to develop and maintain. Interdependence requires active thought plus deliberate *inter*action with others for the purpose of discussing problems, developing and testing ideas, formu-lating plans, and doing and perfecting work. Interdependence requires actively collaborating with and making a contribution to others—the organization, your customers, and your colleagues. At the same time, you are bridging—creating and maintaining—your independence and enhancing a clear sense of yourself. Like the shortstop on a baseball team, you are always a key player, confident about your skill *and* in sync with your team's need.

Stop and think about one great baseball player you've heard of. When he throws the ball to complete a spectacular double play, I doubt that he feels he is giving up anything. He is using his *individual* strength as a component of the *team's* strength. Similarly, when workers are exempted from being part of a team or they feel left out, they don't have a chance to use their skills and make a contribution to the team. When they do participate, they are passing on their strength and making a contribution to others.

Interdependence is rooted in equality—openness and sharing—not subordination—fear and manipulation. Some of my clients, whether management or staff, have figuratively merged with the company they work "for" (dependence); they have no sense of working "with" the organization (independence and interdependence). They have lost their selfness—who they are, separate from the organization. Laid off from her software engineering position, Juanita felt confused but relieved. "The buyout," she said, "gave me a chance to explore who I am and what I want, independent of the company. I was doing whatever my bosses requested, whether I believed in a project or not. I began to see the stark difference between the culture I had come from and the culture the company was becoming. I realized that during the past seven years, *I* had been bought out. My dependence on the company had ruined my self-confidence."

Interdependence is . . .

- collaborating with and supporting others.
- trusting others to support you.
- working toward a goal that challenges you and contributes to your workplace, community, and customers.

More than One Boss or Customer

In my consulting work, I wouldn't think of depending on one client, individual, or organization for my income. First, this is a form of dependence, and in my business I believe dependence is unethical. If I were dependent in my work, I'd be holding on to my clients rather than encouraging their mobility and increasing their productivity. Second, having more than one boss—client—is fascinating and fun. I learn from my clients. What they give to me, I give to other clients. Ming, a management and leadership consultant, said, "In my work, I am helping clients not only to manage change but also to *cause* change. I work with executives, for instance, who are reshaping their companies. Many of these companies are profitable, but today's executives know they can't simply rest on past success. They must learn new skills and attitudes." Ming expanded and reinforced my thinking. I use her notion with my own clients, and now I'm sharing it with you.

If you work at a company, work within as many departments and with as many bosses as you can. If you consult to organizations or coach individuals, expand; select a variety of clients from a range of backgrounds who work in different industries. Your life will be richer and so will theirs. And don't forget that when clients terminate, your company reorganizes, or your boss is fired, you'll go on to have other clients, companies, or bosses who will hire you.

Are you dependent—the old employee-employer contract—or are you negotiating an independent and interdependent path—the new social contract? The following chart will help you see the difference and learn how to make choices.

Dependence or Independence and Interdependence

Seeing the options before you and actively thinking about them are first steps toward choosing between dependence or independence and interdependence. In the left column below is a list of ten characteristics of dependence. In the right column are ten corresponding independent and interdependent characteristics. After you have read one "dependent" characteristic, compare it with the "independent and interdependent" characteristic in the right column. Think about and write down on a separate piece of paper the characteristic that best describes the way you currently see yourself.

Dependent	*Independent and Interdependent*
I seek and wait for approval before committing to action.	I give myself permission to contribute.
I resist new ideas—leave creativity to others.	I create new ideas, options, and projects.
First, I am loyal to my company and customers.	First, I am loyal to myself. If I meet my needs, I can give to others.
I ignore my inner voice. Instead, I put my fate in others' hands.	I listen to and respect my wisdom; I incorporate my knowing into my decision making.
I rarely give thought to matters; mostly I react to conditions.	I engage in active thought and deliberate action.
I keep information to myself.	I readily share information with others.
I am driven by company and client expectations.	I offer my opinions and respect those of others.

—continued

Dependent	Independent and Interdependent
Most of the time, I suppress who I am—sublimate my passion and compromise my values.	I strive to understand and appreciate what I have to contribute and share in a common purpose.
I am apt to manipulate the system—find underhanded ways to get my needs met.	I view myself as resourceful; I negotiate with others to achieve my goals.
Basically, I work for a paycheck.	I work to make a contribution, and I am paid for performance.

On a separate piece of paper, write down one characteristic that you chose as "dependent." Make it a goal within the next month to become conscious of your thoughts and behaviors in this area. Follow through; become more independent and interdependent by discussing with a colleague some ways that you could change your behavior. Barney, a lawyer, for example, felt that the fourth "dependent" characteristic was inhibiting his progress at work. He wrote:

Too often I ignore my inner voice. I defer to the opinions of others.

After a discussion with a friend, Barney decided to take some action steps. He stated them affirmatively:

I will . . .

1. *take fifteen minutes every day to think about what is important to me.*

2. not *judge my solutions to work problems. First, I will write them down and discuss them with a colleague I trust.*

3. *make it a point, at least twice a week, to share my opinions with my boss and colleagues.*

Think of one of your dependent characteristics and write it down. Then name three actions steps you might take toward independence and interdependence.

Serve Yourself to Serve Your Clients and Yourself

Several of my clients are middle-level managers in large corporations who are still gainfully employed. Many have been struggling to survive, trying to adapt to organizations they joined five, ten, or twenty-five years ago that are today unrecognizable. Their jobs are unlikely to last. Some want to learn how they can manage their careers and find or create new jobs within their company. Others are feeling, for personal reasons, that it is time for them to explore options outside of their company—to think beyond what is familiar, to consider their own needs and what they want to contribute to others in the next stage of their lives. This process of giving up familiar territory, overcoming obstacles, and identifying options is painfully difficult for most. They are seeking my support, guidance, and expertise.

One client, Michael, manager of compensation for the division of an automobile manufacturer, called one afternoon with a request: "I'd like to ask you a favor that may at first sound strange." Michael asked if I would call his voice mail at work and leave a supportive message. The message would contain positive, encouraging statements that Michael had heard me use to describe him in past sessions. Michael's ability to know what he needs and to summon the courage to ask for it is unusual and admirable. Particularly for men, asking for help is difficult, because being helped is often interpreted as a weakness. Within half an hour of Michael's request, I left him this message:

Michael,

I want you to truly hear—absorb—this message about you. The most important thing you can do for yourself and for others is to express your authentic self.

This means go for win/win, share your ideas, and listen to others; be a coach—you're a natural at this; use your creativity—you have wonderfully innovative and practical ideas; delegate responsibility—this is your way of trusting others; don't worry about your competence— you're an expert in your field. Mostly, Michael, serve yourself to serve your clients and yourself.

Once they become aware of it, many people with whom I work discover, as Michael did, that they fear their dependence on the organization. They are uncertain about how much of their competence is theirs and how much can be attributed to the organization and others. As a result, they feel despair, gravely questioning their ability to work in another organization or to make some other type of career change. To feel independent and act interdependently, they work hard to free themselves from years of being brainwashed with the notion "Serve the company and it'll serve you." It is anguishing to sift through and wrestle with old messages and expectations. It is challenging and often lonely to go to work and quietly sort through the noise, internally and externally, in order to hear your own voice. If you are fortunate enough to hear it, respect and follow it.

Ask a friend to leave you a voice-mail message. Dial it often. Sit back, take it in.

Be Aware of the "Great Jackass Fallacy"

"The dominant philosophy of motivation in American management is the 'carrot-and-stick philosophy: reward and punishment,' " writes Harry Levinson, management consultant and professor, in *The Great Jackass Fallacy*. When managers in Dr. Levinson's seminars are asked to form a picture in their mind's eye with a carrot at one end and a stick at the other, the managers often identify the "central figure [as] a jackass."

"When the first image that comes to mind when one thinks 'carrot-and-stick' is a jackass," Dr. Levinson writes, "obviously the unconscious assumption behind the reward and punishment model is that one is dealing with jackasses, that people are to be manipulated and controlled. Thus, unconsciously, the boss is the manipulator and controller, and the subordinate is the jackass."[1] If you feel like a jackass long enough, you begin to act like one—stubborn. You consciously or unconsciously come to work late, miss deadlines, blame others, and/or stop volunteering. At this point, you have a chance to reframe "stubborn" as your need for independence. Independence, in this case, does not mean leaving the company or closing the books on your clients or customers. It does, however, refer to the reassessment of your power—your mental and physical ability to stop thinking and acting like a jackass and to begin confronting the obstacles that block your independent thought and action.

You No Longer Work for, You Work *With*

Even in a work world filled with jackasses, now you no longer work *for*, you work *with* a company. Again, *with* implies equality, dignity, and the ability to respond to challenges *as well as* to respect others. If you are someone who works *for*, you frequently ask your boss, "What do you want me to do?" By contrast, it is empowering to work *with* your boss or *with* a team. Your language might change to "I'd like to suggest this as a next step" or "I can identify the problem and, although I don't have any answers yet, I'd like to volunteer to do some research." You might even find that your physical posture changes as well!

With makes a statement about your interdependence: "I've joined the team as a participant in pursuit of a common purpose." *With* is also a statement about your independence: "This is what I have to offer." *With* is a link to the team, project, or organization; it is also a safety net—parachute—and path toward other opportunities. *With* is your new reality. It is a mistake for people to think that they truly work *for* anyone. "At my last job," commented Erik, an engineer, "I believed that I worked for myself and that I was associated with the company. In thinking this way, I felt freer to do my work without preoccupation: What if the company downsizes? Will my job be eliminated?" Instead, Erik has learned to value working *with* the company, doing what needs to be done to serve his customers and colleagues, and attending to his own developmental needs.

I deal every day with people's struggles about dependence on the organization they work *for.* As we have seen, dependent people say, "I have no idea what I would do without my job," "I'd love to leave, but what else would I do?", or "At least I have a job." A dependent business owner might say, "I'll do anything to keep my customers" or "I'll never find another worker like Mike." In part, dependence is common because people neither see nor learn that there are alternatives and that they do have power. Instead, they choose ignorance and excuses.

I grew up believing that "Truth conquers all," and I still follow this maxim. The practical and liberating alternative to dependence combines independence with interdependence. You can be your own person and be part of a team. Remember the flock of migrating geese? Even though others may be tuned in to a dependence frequency or wired to the beat of someone else's music, you don't need to be.

Internal Hierarchies

Over the years, many of us have developed the necessary muscles—intellectual, emotional, and physical—for negotiating hierarchical, that is, superior-subordinate, relationships. The same narrow, top-down arrangement exists internally as well as externally. It is expressed in our self-talk, for example, by "First is better," "Ask permission before you try," and "Fight at any cost to reach the top." Passed on and reinforced by our working predecessors, internalized hierarchies are not easy to examine. We must challenge and rearrange the framework of "carrots and sticks"—rewards and punishments.

Our parents reminded us, "Be good and you can go first." Our teachers said, "If you raise your hand first with the *right* answer, you'll be rewarded." Our bosses insisted, "If you do what you're told and deliver, you'll be paid." Our internal hierarchies reflect what we have been taught—dependence on a system; we are controlled by the notion of reward and punishment. I've had clients say to me, "If I'm not promoted, I'll leave," as if there were no other choices. Like dependent children, they pout, and some run away.

The hierarchy also keeps us focused on the organization's mission and goals, with little attention to our own. Who has the time to attend to—much less reward us for—our goals? "Competition was the name of the game, but one day I woke up to my needs," commented Jill, a territory sales supervisor. Now I job-share with Sandra, another supervisor; we each work part-time."

On one thing, wives and husbands agree: Unemployment has changed their outlook forever, whether or not the men find work. Gone, most strikingly, is the blind corporate loyalty that sustained them through 14-hour days and repeated relocations.

—Tony Horwitz, "Jobless Male Managers Proliferate in Suburbs, Cause Subtle Malaise," **Wall Street Journal**

Self-Control

Narrow, rigid hierarchies, fed by unbridled growth, have depended predominantly on the wisdom of the "superiors." In these uncharted times, the economic, spiritual, and physical fate of individuals and organizations can no longer be placed into the hands of superiors. Their strength may be admirable and helpful, but alone it is limiting. The involvement and contribution of others—your vision and expertise—have become essential. "I'm a 'utility player,' " said Melanie, a systems analyst. "I go where the problems are and use my abilities to manage, lead, and implement. I used to see myself as someone who would do anything necessary to climb the stovepipe to the top. The company that I worked *for* reinforced this, and I bought in. My MBA served as a competitive weapon. The company has been slow to change, but today it seems they respect my versatility more and I feel liberated by my awareness that other organizations might also need my skills."

For Melanie, self-control replaced being controlled. Internally, she replaced the image of climbing a stovepipe with that of ascending a willow tree—well rooted, distinctive, and flexible. She is able to grow, stand firm, bend, and sway. Her MBA is no longer a weapon but a symbolic reminder of her ability to learn and to continue learning.

Andre, a training coordinator with talent and passion in the applied arts, was still blocked by the stovepipe—the traditional ladder—*in his mind*. When he talked about turning his artistic talents into a business, initially he glowed, but quickly his glow was diminished by premature, unexamined judgment. "Who would buy my work?" he asked. "Besides, there are a lot of great artists out there." I said to Andre, "Yes, there are great artists out there, and, like you, they have to learn to recognize *their* greatness."

Listed below are different ways we think about our work. As you can see, the statements in the left column illustrate rigid, dependent ways of thinking. In the right column, the statements show more flexibility and independence. Note the statements that most accurately reflect your beliefs. Be careful not to judge yourself as you review your answers. Use this exercise as a learning tool.

It's important to . . .

▤ be first.	≡ be involved.
▤ move up.	≡ contribute.
▤ know *the* answer.	≡ know the questions.
▤ ask the boss.	≡ seek another's opinion, not permission.
▤ change only when necessary.	≡ look at alternatives, experiment.
▤ be rewarded.	≡ reward yourself.

If you're willing to take risks and accept responsibility, you can have equality and dignity.

You can . . .

≡ speak your mind, volunteer solutions, and initiate meetings.

≡ prioritize your values and live them.

≡ rewrite your job description, and apply for or create a new job.

≣ use your abilities in a different company.

≣ become your own boss—you are anyway.

≣ develop new services and sell to different customers.

≣ analyze what makes you a top performer.

≣ set new goals and be joyful about achieving them.

Integrating independence and interdependence takes effort, and it works. It starts, evolves, and continues with *you*.

Lemons into Lemonade: One Person Makes a Difference

Hartman and Clark (a fictitious name) is a commercial real estate firm that was structured hierarchically in the 1980s; workers at all levels had bosses and the bosses had the answers: It was a dependent worker system. Today the company has hired a consulting firm to guide the executives through a culture change, a process that will flatten the company and change the ways people think and work. This process involves assembling workers into teams of specialists—experts collaborating with one another to improve service to customers. Hartman and Clark will soon be an interdependent workplace. Hartman and Clark's reorganization effort is aimed at creating a new, nonhierarchical structure in which all workers will be responsible for their individual productivity *and* their team's productivity. A revised compensation plan will reflect the change: Individuals will be paid a salary, and each team will receive a bonus based on performance.

Clive, one of the senior partners, called me and said, "We have a couple of people in the firm who have been valuable players, but I'm not sure if they can change as our organization does. I'm *not* convinced that they need to go; that's why I'm calling you. I want to change this company *and* help people to make changes *with* us." We met and decided that I would begin to coach Anthony, a financial analyst who had been with the firm for several years and who Clive thought might have difficulty adapting to the team approach.

First I interviewed Brent, Anthony's boss. Brent summarized Anthony's problem: "He's just not an effective team player." Surprisingly, in my initial conversation with Anthony, he saw doing some "career work" as an opportunity, one he had thought about in the past but had needed a push to act on. Anthony liked his work and felt he was well suited to his role. Regarding cultural fit, he remarked, "Most of the people in my division are more expressive than I am—they are sales types. I like to work *alone* on projects to get the job done. I also like to think that my work speaks for itself, unlike my colleagues, who frequently announce, 'Look what I just accomplished.' " Toward the close of our meeting I assured Anthony that he would learn a great deal from the coaching process. "Anthony," I said, "you will build your confidence, and you will be able to make sense of information that can be very helpful as you make choices and changes."

Our plan for Anthony included his taking two career inventories, the Myers-Briggs Type Indicator (MBTI) and the Johnson O'Connor Inventory of Aptitudes and Knowledge (JOIAK). The MBTI gives people information about their personality type, information that can be used to make effective career or job decisions and to help people better understand their communication style. The JOIAK helps people discover or affirm their aptitudes, or natural talents (musical and artistic talent are examples of aptitudes).

After completing the inventories, Anthony received feedback from each diagnostic specialist on my team. Anthony invited Kim, his wife, to join him at our meetings. She provided support, and her own experience with Anthony affirmed some of the observations we had made. In my practice, every client who sits across from me is not sitting alone. Each is part of a larger, interconnected system. During our first meeting, although Anthony physically sat alone, across from me, I was aware that his wife, children, parents, boss, and other people in his life, past and present, as well as societal expectations and mortgage payments, were also present and influencing his choices and behaviors. This is the case for all of us; even when we are alone, we are not alone.

Anthony discovered that his aptitude with numbers and tonal memory lent themselves naturally to his work with facts and figures—validation for what he already knew. He learned through the MBTI that his natural tendency was to relate more to the world of ideas (introversion) than to the outer world of people (extraversion). Kim, an extravert, pointed out that she had reminded him of this fact several times throughout their marriage. His introverted nature, although different from that of many in his division (and that of his wife), did not make him better or worse than others, just different. And Anthony's style was part of what he uniquely brought to his team. His task was to learn how to communicate more effectively with his colleagues so that he would be understood and their needs would be met. As Anthony said, most of his team members preferred to talk frequently about their accomplishments. Different communication styles didn't mean they weren't a team; they had a common purpose—to serve the customer. Anthony learned he could communicate with them and respect his own, more introverted style by writing and sending a weekly update memo to each team member.

Anthony remarked, "There are two primary concerns at work—one, the way teams are evaluated for compensation, and two, what people will do if they don't get along with team members." Anthony smiled and said, "I was dealt a handful of lemons, and I'm turning them into lemonade for myself and others." Clarifying his personality type and confirming his aptitudes demonstrated to Anthony the power of knowing himself (an ongoing process) in a changing system. He did not have to be a victim, but he could become a player again.

With encouragement from his wife, with renewed spirit, and with clarification and new words to explain his attributes, Anthony arranged a meeting with Clive and Brent. He brought three key points to the table: He thanked Clive and Brent for the opportunity to learn about himself, he told them what he had learned and what the process involved, and he proposed that they encourage others to go through the same process. Following this meeting, Clive and Brent made a commitment to support other individuals in the organization to learn about their communication styles. Their aim was to help Anthony's colleagues benefit from increased self-knowledge too, and then apply that knowledge to be able to work more productively together. With a more aware and functional team of workers, Clive and Brent could now expect to see increased revenues as a result.

Clive and Brent learned that the notion of having a "perfect" team of clones is not the answer to the need for improved productivity and is at best a temporary solution. Changing team members, a fluctuating marketplace, and increasing competition call for flexible, multiskilled teams. When workers at Hartman and Clark learned about their aptitudes and communication styles, that knowledge gave them personal power to make changes and helped them to communicate more effectively with one another. Good teams have members with complementary skills who respect one another's differences.

Successful "organizational" redeveloping cannot occur without "personal" redeveloping—people learning to become more independent and interdependent. That's where Anthony, Hartman and Clark, and the world of work are headed. We are all taking responsibility for discovering who we are and for making a contribution to others.

Career Enhancement, Not Only Advancement

Career/job "enhancement" is an ongoing process of self-development, career planning, productivity, and contribution that neither precludes nor depends on career/job "advancement." The traditional career ladder is the obvious career/job advancement choice, but, as discussed earlier, now that organizations are flattening, the ladder approach is less available. The concept of enhancement puts the onus on you to do your skills inventory, notice needs in your organization, and identify your customer's needs. If you choose enhancement, you will be challenged rather than restricted by the limits of advancement. You will actively seek opportunities.

Paradoxically, as you enhance, you are likely to advance. If you choose enhancement, you will challenge the "one-boss advancement" model. "I used to accept a new job because I believed in the boss and because the advancement opportunities looked good," said Gary, director of quality control at a hospital. "Basically, I trusted my boss and behaved as though he would pull me up the ladder as *he* was promoted." Gary's career values have shifted. "Today, I look at the bigger picture. My boss was fired, and so was I. Looking back, I hadn't gotten involved enough. I knew only a small circle of people and focused on doing the tasks that I thought would give me visibility [promotability]." Dependence, as illustrated by Gary's singular focus on advancement, is a vulnerable state. If something happened to your boss or your career track, what would you do?

By identifying contacts in or outside of your organization, you can collect important information—company goals, new product reviews, job leads—for your career enhancement. Your task, after writing down some names, is to network—gather information. Networking is the active development and careful use of contacts for personal and professional development. It is *not* for the purpose of job interviewing. Some of my clients complain that many company contacts are refusing to grant informational interviews, and I suspect the reason is partially that job seekers have become more manipulative—they ask for one thing but do another.

Self-Respect: A Case Study

"My boss might ask me to do twenty things, and I might get nineteen of them right," exclaimed Jolienne, a compensation specialist. "She then berates me for my *one* mistake. This happens constantly. I know it's not just me—she scolds other staff in the same way. The longer I stay at my job, the more I'm losing respect for myself." When I asked Jolienne why she had not done something to change her situation, she initially said it was because the job was part-time, she had a three-year-old son, and she wanted time with him. Ultimately, she uncovered a deeper reason: She believed it would be nearly impossible to find a part-time job in her field, let alone one she would enjoy.

I asked Jolienne if she had ever experienced similar conflicts. She had—at a previous job, and in her relationship with her mother. "In my old job, I grew intolerant of my supervisor's put-downs and packed my bags. Regarding my mother, I was the one in my family to challenge her criticisms; my brother and sister would sit back while I'd talk back. It didn't do much good; to this day, my mother still criticizes us. So I handle the situation by visiting my parents as little as possible, maybe once or twice a year."

Jolienne doubted that her work life could be different, that she could choose a boss who would encourage her and treat her with dignity. I said, "You can have your doubts, but please leave a little opening for the possibility that you *can* become independent and choose healthier work relationships." She began to recognize the ways that she had become dependent on—grown accustomed to—a demeaning type of relationship. In addition, she was able to identify times when she *had* chosen healthier relationships, ones in which she had preserved her dignity by speaking up.

Over time, Jolienne talked more about her doubts and her unhealthy relationships, as well as about her positive choices. She began to deepen her understanding of what was important to her and what to look for in other people. For example, she had strong intuitive skills and claimed that she could sense the type of boss who would not be a good match for her. She didn't always trust her intuition, however. I asked her, "Would you give me an example of something your current boss says or does that you would characterize as demeaning?" She answered, "She says things like, 'Do it. I don't want any questions,' or she will ask, 'What do you think?' but then walk away as I'm answering. Or she will constantly say, 'I want you to ask me before you do anything.' "

Eventually Jolienne reframed the negative message "I can't trust my intuition." She called her intuition "my best friend; someone I can trust." "A best friend," she declared, "listens. Sometimes they say nothing at all, but their presence gives me courage and faith in myself." I asked her, "Is there anyone in your life who depends on your intuition?" She gleamed and said, "My son. When he cries, I just know what he needs." "What do you mean?" I asked. Her reply? "I trust [listen to] my intuition."

Next Jolienne began to think of several situations at work when she had trusted her intuition. She had offered a troubled colleague timely help, for example, and once she had chosen the name for one of the company's new products. I then asked her, "When you think of times when your intuition has been your 'best friend,' how did you behave? What would I see you doing?" "I asked people questions and volunteered solutions," she responded. "Often I was the first to come up with new ideas." I asked, "When you did not trust your intuition, how did you behave?" "I kept to myself," she replied.

※

Reframing Changes Behavior

Old Frame	Reframe
Thought: I can't trust my intuition.	My intuition is my best friend.
Behavior: Withdraws, closes down.	Contributes, questions, volunteers solutions.

While Jolienne was in the process of looking for another job, I continued to encourage her to take on a "self-employed" attitude—to integrate independence (clarify what she needed) and interdependence (understand the needs and operative style of a boss and team that she might be joining). She gradually learned to honor her intuitive perception, to ask pointed questions, and to listen acutely to the response. In one interview, she asked a prospective boss, "Would you give me several examples of how you work with your staff?" Notice that she did not say, "Would you tell me about the times when you have *collaborated* with your staff?" Saying "collaborated" might have cued the interviewer about Jolienne's own values. She would share these later on in the interview. The neutral question is open-ended and allows for a more objective answer. When Jolienne finally found a new part-time position, she had interviewed not only the boss but the staff as well. She did not ask the staff if their boss was fair, open, direct, or flexible. Instead, she asked staff members to describe the ways in which the boss operated. Again, it was critical not to indicate any bias in her inquiry; she gave the staff minimal cues about what she was looking for, in order to elicit responses she could trust.

Jolienne learned to think and act independently and eventually found a work situation where interdependent relationships prevailed, including the one between her and her boss.

We will experience our freedom the moment we take our assignment, our job, and make it our own.

—*Peter Block,* **Stewardship: Choosing Service over Self-Interest**

Some Signs That You Are Integrating Independence and Interdependence

You are developing . . .

- an ability to move beyond your fears.
- a loyalty to "self-truth."
- a sense that you can make a difference.
- a willingness to plan and take risks.
- a facility to manage outcomes.
- a spirit of adventure.
- an attitude of support for others on their journey.
- a loss of interest in controlling others.
- a freedom to give and to receive.

As you learn to become more independent and interdependent, you will gain greater satisfaction from your work and feel more alive and productive. In the next chapter, you will discover that joining— working *with*—others is at the core of this notion.

4

JOINING, NOT WORKING FOR, YOUR ORGANIZATION AND CUSTOMERS

*Build work and work relationships
based on equality and competence*

EMPLOYED ATTITUDE

Dependent Mindset

I am enmeshed with the company and customers; I work for them. Whether I agree or not, I do what is expected of me.

SELF-EMPLOYED ATTITUDE

Independent and Interdependent Mindset

I will join, not work for, my organization and customers. I provide a service based on equality and competence, whether I work in or outside the organization.

W HEN I RECALL MY MOST ENJOYABLE AND PRODUC- TIVE WORK EXPERIENCES, I think of times when I felt strongly about what I was doing and when I was work- ing with peers. Peers are those with whom we have an equal relation- ship and for whom we have great respect. "Peer work" occurs when we join with a person, a group, or an organization for a shared pur- pose—a joint venture of equals. We listen and are listened to, we share our ideas and consider the ideas of others, we give constructive criti- cism and receive feedback from others, and everyone maintains his or her dignity in the process. I had this experience most recently while writing this book. After I wrote the first draft, the publisher, Berrett- Koehler, and I sent copies to several reviewers. Although I did not know most of the reviewers, I considered their feedback and the care they put into formulating their feedback an invaluable peer review. Each reviewer wrote me and Berrett-Koehler a comprehensive letter describing what she or he would change in the manuscript.

Ralph Katz, a friend and a sales and management consultant, was one of the reviewers. Ralph questioned the original subject of this chapter, the notion of "partnering" with your organization. Ralph felt that for most workers today, the notion of partnering was rigid, too permanent. He challenged me to think in terms of *peer* relationships and their influence on healthy working relationships. After careful thought, I revised the chapter to include Ralph's suggestion. Thanks in part to my peer relationship with him, this chapter explores some thoughts about peer work and ways it could work for you.

Peer Work

Peer work—joining others for a shared purpose—is built on the fundamental requirement of equality. Few of us want to feel "less than" another person (a boss) with whom we work. Most of us want to be able to share our ideas, work with others toward common goals, and have equality in the process. We want to establish this peer relationship with our fellow workers, our suppliers, and our customers.

The clients I work with who are most fulfilled enjoy this kind of relationship with their organization, customers, and colleagues while working toward a goal. They make contributions, using their authentic selves in the process, and in return they are challenged, recognized, and rewarded. They benefit from joint satisfaction gained over a period of time.

Peer work entails an ongoing process of learning, negotiating, and contributing. A finished project becomes a catalyst toward a deeper relationship and other opportunities. Two consultants, for example, coauthored an article; their next project is a book. Joining each other does *not* mean drafting a document that requires a two-party signature or a debate over whose name will appear in larger print. Peer work *is* a joint activity undertaken by two or more people with common interests, mutual respect, and goals that lead to effective outcomes. It is a *process* rather than a legal structure, and it can be created with others, at different levels, in your organization. Joining your organization in today's scrutinizing and cost-conscious work climate, where at any time you could be viewed as an asset or a liability, requires wisdom, hard work, and patience.

My brother Chris, a rheumatologist, runs a peer practice. He serves his patients by practicing involvement—actively giving to and learning from his patients. Chris and his staff share their ideas and observations in an effort to deliver quality service. In another case, Linda, an Olympics hopeful, practices swimming laps on most days of the year. Her coach encourages and guides her. They join each other, with the vision that Linda will qualify for the Olympics. In a corporate setting, Herb Landsman, senior merchandise manager at T. J. Maxx, believes, "You have to build bridges with people and find a common ground. You must ask yourself, 'What kinds of relationships am I creating?' The win is in the interpersonal win, it's in the trust . . . bonding relationships as you are employed."

The following page shows a comparison between the essential elements of working for—subordinating yourself—and joining—peer work.

Reframing the Way You Work

At this point, you might be thinking, "Peer work—where *I* work, between me and *my* company? Impossible!" But I am not talking about a partnership—a formal title and position. Rather, I am suggesting joining—a flexible, expansive activity in which you engage in problem solving and commit to going ahead. "Going ahead" is an hour-to-hour decision for some, and for others it is a daily mantra to put their best effort into whatever job they are doing. You could be looking for a job, redefining your current job, addressing a customer's complaint, or figuring out how to launch your company's next product. Joining is a component of your "self-employed" attitude whereby you overcome your resistance to change and involve yourself in the business at hand. You do not allow yourself to be pulled downstream; you use your imagination, energy, and skill to solve problems—swim ahead—and become part of the solution.

⚓

Are You "Working for" or "Joining"?

Compare the column on the left with the one on the right and note the behavior that best describes what you do. Remember, seeing your current behavior can become a springboard for change.

Working For *Subordinating Yourself*	Joining *Peer Work*
Looking "up" for direction and most of the answers.	Questioning, collaborating, and negotiating with others to discover common ground and develop solutions.
Staying put when feeling apathetic about company values, services, and/or products.	Owning your own values and feeling genuinely aligned with the company's vision and goals.
Accepting and doing the same repetitive work.	Learning new processes and contributing to colleagues and customers.
Waiting for others to plan your career.	Initiating and continuing your personal and professional growth.
Seeing others primarily as a boss and/or a competitor.	Creating relationships built on mutual respect and common purpose, support, and the exchange of information.

Peer Work: A Risk Worth Taking

Making a daily investment in doing your best is at the very least a challenge when you face the possibility of losing your job at any moment. Bonnie, a project director at a nonprofit agency, said, "My general tendency is to protect myself—to do only what needs to be done to get by." This posture will not work in today's work world. Paradoxically, Bonnie's *lack* of commitment and energy would most likely be noticed, and she could lose her job.

"This is difficult," remarked Maya, a sales manager with a consumer products company, "especially when my head is engaged but my heart isn't in it. My company has been laying off people in droves, and I know I could be next. At the same time, even though I'm losing some of my fight, I try to hold on to the bigger picture and believe that my contribution will make a difference." Maya, one of my clients, is putting a tremendous amount of energy into her current work, and at the same time she is developing what she refers to as "plan B." Peer work, for Maya, is not a process of blind devotion but one that is grounded in doing her work *and* developing alternatives. Using her plan B, she can be loyal to herself *and* to the workers on her team by examining her skills and their relevancy to both her workplace and the broader market. Maya's goal is to be able to understand clearly and articulate her role, regardless of the work setting. She can't afford to "put all her eggs in one basket."

Maya's Plan B

Self-Assessment and Seeing the Bigger Picture

Skills identification and values clarification
- What are my core skills and which are most valued?
- Have my values changed? Which values are my priorities?

Clarification of work role
- In what ways does my work meet my needs?
- What parts of my work are relevant to the needs of my customers?

Networking for information and ideas
- Of the people I've talked with in the past month, whose work interests me?

≣ What have I gained from talking with people in other
organizations and professional areas?

Expression of my needs and what I can contribute
≣ Do I share with my boss that I'm looking for new challenges?
≣ Do I inform my boss about my accomplishments?

When You "Join," Know Your Customers

Customers are individuals or organizations that benefit from your interaction with them. Every stage of production or service involves a customer. The person sitting next to you is your customer; you get
paid—indirectly or directly—to serve him or her. Who is sitting next to
you—a manager? a salesperson? an assembler? a programmer? a secretary? a stockholder? an employer? Your customer may be depending on
you for up-to-date stock information, a final draft of a report, or a satisfactory assembly-line inspection.

People working at all levels inside organizations, even the president, have customers. The president must satisfy the stockholders and
ultimately answer to the buyer. If enough buyers are dissatisfied, the
president will be held accountable and may lose customers and, possibly, his or her job. The sales manager also has customers, both the
sales staff and you, the buyer of the product or service. And the
administrative assistant has one or more customers, including a manager and other staff who need backup support. In each case, the continuity of the customer-worker relationship depends on the recognition
and satisfaction of the customer's needs. If a high-tech company manu-
factures small-screen computers and the customer wants one with a
large screen, the company needs to adapt or the customer will buy
elsewhere. And if the manager promises the salesperson to deliver in
one week a large-screen computer and there is a delay, the manager
will then need to deal with the disgruntled customer.

Neiman Marcus, the Texas-based retailer, knows its customers pay for service. Workers there serve the customer better by using an "inter-cell" system. Sales associates in the cosmetics department, for example, assist customers by moving freely between one specialized area— cell—and another. Ongoing product and service training keeps sales associates informed and committed to their goal: serving the customer.

Peer Work Requires Relevancy

As Jack Welch, chairman of General Electric Corporation, wrote in *Fortune* in 1993, "[Success is] a matter of understanding the customer's needs instead of just making something and putting it into a box. It's a matter of seeing the importance of your role in the total process."[1] Frederick, the editor of an executive newsletter, gets paid for delivering timely, practical advice to his professional readership. He also gets paid to ask his readers about their ideas and interests and to communicate those ideas and interests to other journalists. In addition, he frequently asks his staff about their ideas and insights. In a nutshell, he gathers and synthesizes information and manages and consults with his staff in an effort to deliver succinct, worthwhile information. He will continue to get paid if the newsletter meets the needs of his readership. Frederick commented, "My work must be germane to my readership. The readers must be benefiting from my actions or I wouldn't get paid—I could possibly lose my job; worst case, this publication could go down the tubes."

We can see ourselves as workers who accept and do the same old repetitive work or as contributors who add to the profitability of the company by delivering a valued service to the customer. But it is not enough simply to *do* or to *sell* your product or service. You must first conduct research to determine if your proposal or service will satisfy the customer. In Maya's case, for example, she manages a group of salespeople and was planning to present a program to them on how to close a sale. But first she asked the staff members—her peers—what *they* wanted to learn, and they said they would benefit more from a program on how to listen. Therefore, Maya's first plan would have been irrelevant, and so she reassessed the relevancy of her first proposal and redesigned her training seminar accordingly.

For job seekers, the art of peer work—matching skill with customer—is essential. The prospective customer or employer will undoubtedly wonder, "How can this person I am interviewing solve my problems?" Be prepared to give examples of what you do that can be useful to *your* customer or potential employer. A "self-employed" attitude requires a plan B, the ongoing examination of your skills and values and the practice of using them to address the needs of different customers.

Howard, a graduate student and career changer, felt a lack of focus in his new studies in health care management. Howard had invested his time and money to develop his skills. His general goal was to find work that would utilize his education and interests. Previously, he had managed the family wholesale carpet business. He was upset because he wasn't sure that school was meeting his career needs. It was, however, a place where he could hang his hat on a daily basis. It kept him busy and focused, but ultimately out of touch with the world of work.

As we explored his concerns, Howard identified a gap in his career development process: He had been accepted into the program, but he had not talked with people in the health care management field about how they had applied their education and experience to their current situation. Howard concluded that he needed to network so that he could better understand how his previous work experience could be combined with his education to establish a specific career goal. School is not an "answer," but it can be a valuable asset and credential, especially as you clarify what you bring to the marketplace and how you can apply your unique skills and talents.

You Can Meet Your Needs and Your Customers' Needs

Whether you are employed full- or part-time, changing careers, laid-off and looking for the same type of work, never-want-to-retire, or a recent college graduate, your success will be contingent on matching your skills and interests with customers' needs. You will create a job, retain your current job, or find a new job only if you are adding value to customers.

Think about the following questions, and answer them to the best of your ability. Feel free to discuss your thoughts and answers with a colleague.

What do you specifically do to meet your customers' or potential employer's needs?
Example: I ask a question before I offer a solution.

How do you know when your customers, employer, or the person with whom you are interviewing is satisfied?
Example: I know my customers are satisfied when they request a repeat order as a result of my thorough and accurate research regarding their concerns about the product.

Identifying Your Customers

"Who are my customers, anyway?" I could not answer this question any better than by quoting Marsha Selva, president and travel consultant, Here Today, There Tomorrow Travel. She stated:

My customers are my profit.
I am overhead, they are profit.

To identify your customers try answering the following questions. Before you write, think about who your customers are and what you specifically do to provide service.

How do you define your customers?
Example: My customers are typically professionals with a college education and ten or more years of work experience. They are dissatisfied with some aspect of their career or work and are seeking my guidance and coaching in order to progress through their career transition or resolve their work issue.

What are some of your customers' needs?
Example: A primary need of my customers is to talk about their work experience and to sort out and make decisions about what skills they want to use in the next stage of their career.

I help people [customers] to understand my role. I share why I do what I'm doing, and I work together to create negotiated outcomes.

—Debbie Hicks, manager of human resources, Harvard Community Health Plan of New England

Face Your Customers

Add value. That's your basic goal. Workers are evaluated by their customers, not merely by faceless organizations. Every worker—president, vice-president, manager, and staff—reports to the customer. And so when you propose an idea to a group, present a business plan to a banker, or interview for a job, the question behind *their* questions is, "What value will you add?" In other words, how will you benefit the customer?

If you've done your inner work—assessed who you are and what you want—your next step is to harness your resources in such a way that they'll add value to the customer. Lisa, the scriptwriter, did this when she answered the question, "What will others buy from me?" Another career changer, Helen, a former lawyer, found that she was a historian at heart. Helen combined her love for the classics, her law background, and her ability to write. She first clarified and prioritized her own needs, then identified a historical consulting firm. In her new role, she researches and writes histories of corporations. Before she arrived at this company, no one at the firm had provided these services. In essence, she created a niche that has meaning for her *and* attracts and serves the customer.

It won't work for job seekers, career changers, workers within organizations, or consultants to solicit jobs today. To reach your goal successfully, you must share ideas and demonstrate how you can serve the customer. Organizations can't afford to hire the wrong person, and customers are the key rule makers: "Provide quality services and products at a fair price or I'll go elsewhere."

Have you done your research? If not, it's nearly impossible to know how you'll add value. Start by looking for a job that you'd *like* or by analyzing a problem in or outside of your company that you would like to work on. Ask a librarian for research assistance, and read everything you can get your hands on about the organization: its place in the market sector, the outside forces that influence its business, and what makes people successful in your chosen professional area. If you are researching a company, for example, find out who the customers are, what products and/or services they have bought, who the competition is, and what the organizational culture is like.

In your search, if you always keep in mind that *your* job is to match your abilities and interests with the needs of the customer, then you will achieve your goal: to find a meaningful job, start a business, create a niche, or lead a company.

◪

I'm my own employer. CRM is my customer.
—*Kirby Timmons, creative director, CRM Films*

Active Joining

Current times call for a different mindset: *active joining*, a process in which you, the individual, the learning-to-be-self-employed contributor, are asking questions, sharing ideas, and putting energy into solving problems and serving your customer, colleague, and organization. Simply stated, achieving your goals will involve active alliances—peer relationships—within the new, flatter workplace. The organization requires your initiative and input when hierarchical barriers are removed. I've heard countless "bosses" say, "I want people to come forward with what they want to do. Very few workers take the initiative. They play it safe."

The *concept* of active joining isn't new. For most of you, its newness will probably be in the *practice*. The ongoing advancements in aviation, computers, and agriculture, for example, grew out of the active joining of resources between government and private enterprise. Each member took risks and contributed expertise. Each member learned to be open to the other's ideas, thereby creating the inspiration and resources for better products and services. On a smaller scale, one such collaborative effort is the High Technology Center, in Wilmington,

Massachusetts. The High Technology Center is a career transition service that was developed by joining the resources of Wang Laboratories, General Electric, Industrial Services Program, and the University of Massachusetts. Their joint commitment is to provide the job seeker with a positive professional environment in which to conduct a productive reemployment campaign.

Active joining is the process of creating a bridge between what you believe, do, and contribute and your organization's, customer's, or client's needs. The beauty of active joining is in the way that people take the initiative and participate in developing creative answers to problems in the workplace. For instance, Carlos, a hospital administrator, thought, "How can I develop and sell new programs to community groups?" Developing and selling the programs, he discovered, would probably work best through actively joining the groups. Carlos gave himself permission to experiment.

To begin, he made a list of the community groups that he thought would benefit most from preventive health care programs. Next, he clearly defined and wrote down his proposed ideas and read them aloud to a colleague. Carlos then called each client and said something like, "I'd like to develop some new preventive health care services that will better serve your group. Your input is vital. Would you and a small group from your organization be willing to meet with me? The purpose of the meeting would be for our organization to learn about some of your needs and ideas and to share some of ours. I plan to meet with five other community groups. I'd be happy to review my collective findings with you in exchange for your time and insights."

In effect, Carlos created a bridge between community groups (one customer) and his organization (another customer). He took the initiative to develop and expand services for his main customer, the hospital.

He asked what his community customers needed and shared those needs with his colleagues, eventually developing tailored programs that were of mutual benefit.

Mobilizing Workers: Retaining Won't Work

As a consultant to organizations, I often hear, "Our problem is that we have to figure out a strategy for retaining employees. We've downsized and can't afford to lose any more employees. Can you write a proposal outlining how to do this?" My answer is, "I could, but I won't." Retaining workers (my term!) doesn't make sense in a mobile world. Flexibility, knowledge, challenge, and clarity do. Instead, I recommend that the organization create a program focused on career self-development and management for workers at all levels, a program that provides support and tools for all workers to know themselves better and to make personal and professional decisions and contributions. Companies need to *earn* the devotion, loyalty, and energy of their workers. Some contemporary examples include Starbucks, Bread and Circus, T. J. Maxx, Lotus Development Corporation, the Body Shop, Polaroid, and Nordstrom's.

The word *retain* means to "keep one's position" or to "hold in one place." An image comes to mind of a retaining wall, a structure designed to keep at bay a formidable force. Retaining devices and systems do not guarantee organizational stability and productivity; we need to encourage joining—peer work—as a design for individual and team development and productivity.

The Sides Are Spreading as You Read This

In today's marketplace, organizations must first work toward survival. Survival will rest largely on respecting the fact that the hierarchy, a rigid top-down system, is quickly perishing. Horizontal organizations—

those involving team participation—once novel, are emerging. At their core, such organizations respect each individual's valuable skills and potential for contribution.

It will not be enough to rely on experts. Ordinary citizens must become experts too. It will take public opinion on a wide scale to ensure that world leaders act.

—Mikhail Gorbachev, quoted in Parade

The top, so to speak, is learning to join you. Those at the top are learning to share their problems and look for answers among you, the experts. On December 9, 1993, the *Wall Street Journal* reported, "Xerox has been asking its workers to find ways to increase productivity. Assembly-line workers have evaluated how they could achieve their work faster and better and have taken small steps toward their goals." The renewed organization can't afford excess "baggage" and can't afford *not* to recognize and utilize the talent of every one of its workers. Nor can the workers in any organization allow themselves to go unrecognized. These points are central to the notion that "we are all self-employed" and to the collaboration between individual and organization. The July 1993 cover story of *Inc.* magazine, "Employers of the Year," cites examples of "workplaces employees love," successful businesses in a variety of industries ranging from health care to manufacturing to software:

≣ **Fitcorp.** Fitness-Center Operator, 80 employees, $8.5 million in sales, Boston.
Offers a parallel-track career path for staffers who wish to build skills but don't want to move into management.

≣ **Stonyfield Farm.** Yogurt Manufacturer, 87 employees, $12 million in sales, Londonderry (N.H.).
Clearly communicates career-growth opportunities to all employees. Promotes competent learners.

≣ **Action Instruments.** Instrument Manufacturer, 200 employees, $25 million in sales, San Diego.
Urges employees to "make it happen," to solve problems that they discover. Sets loose boundaries to define scope of autonomy. Engenders self-motivation through open-book financial disclosure.

≣ **Job Boss Software.** Developer of Factory Software, 40 employees, $2.3 million in sales, Minneapolis.
Encourages employees to take ownership of their jobs. Hires rigorously, trains well, and then grants employees wide latitude. Has managers who act more like facilitators than bosses.[2]

These organizations join—work *with*—the individuals who work with them.

To break tradition and embrace a new culture of change, the company's executives have gathered in a classroom. . . . They're debating the wisdom of challenging the boss. "I can disagree all the way up to the president," claims one manager.

—Lori Bongiorno, "Corporate America's New Lesson Plan," **Business Week**

Joining: Individual Mobility and Organizational Productivity

It is a false premise that any organization can retain its best workers, as if people and events could be manipulated and success guaranteed so long as the company kept and controlled the right people in the right places. A project that you're working on today can be terminated tomorrow, through no fault of your own. Your workplace is a microcosm of the external marketplace. Yesterday's success is a weak predictor of tomorrow's outcomes. Competition between Olympic athletes can remind us of this notion.

It's not enough for an organization to reward 10 percent of its workforce in the hope that they will stay put, make things productive, or guarantee success. Workers at all levels must develop a "self-managed career." This concept is an essential aspect of joining. You'll be joining, for example, when you ask for meetings with your boss instead of waiting to be summoned, when you decide on a training program or course that you think would benefit your career mobility and your company's productivity, when you discuss that program's relevancy with your boss and then ask her or him to consider it as a budget item. And you'll be joining when you ask a prospective employer to provide you with its customers' names so that you can talk with them before you make a decision about accepting a new job. One outcome of career self-management is mobility—the ability to see and seek alternatives and to make choices that benefit you, the worker, and your organization or customer.

Peer Work—Career Development Review

Peer work—a design for individual and team development and productivity—involves a career development review, at least once a year, for workers at all levels. Such a review would be initiated by the organization, and it would be the responsibility of all workers to arrange a meeting with their boss to discuss their past development activities and future development plans.

All workers would be prepared to . . .

≣   briefly summarize the development activities (training, special programs, counseling) they had been involved in during the previous twelve months.

≣   discuss the contributions they had made to their department, customers, and organization during the previous twelve months.

≣   comment on how any extracurricular activities had influenced their career and performance during the previous twelve months.

≣   identify the types of activities and responsibilities they would like to have more of in their current and future work.

≣   list and discuss personal qualities and job skills they would like to work on during the upcoming twelve months to improve their present job performance and to achieve their personal career goals.

The organization would join the workers by . . .

≣   creating "compensation bands," flexible reward systems that support job development and movement—the lattice—commensurate with individual worker needs and organizational goals.

≣   respecting all individuals for their courage to initiate, participate, grow, and change; and by honoring the confidentiality of personal information.

≣   providing career development resources (books, inventories, special programs, learning forums, counsel) for individuals.

≣   posting internal job opportunities and encouraging workers to interview for those positions.

≣   staying open and flexible to worker transition as a necessary part of the development and productivity process.

The tool on the following page can be used by you and your organization for career planning purposes. Share it with your boss and other workers. Use it during your career development review or at any other stage of your process as a guide for optimizing your career success and productivity. If you are between jobs or looking for your first job, follow this plan or adapt it in ways that serve your purposes.

▟▙

Career Action Plan

Career Self-Management

This plan will help you to clarify your goal and identify the methods you'll use and the steps you'll take to achieve it.

In discussion with a colleague or on your own, first write down one goal (A) that you'd like to achieve (e.g., close a sale, run a collaborative meeting, learn a new accounting procedure). Second, clarify the benefits to you and your customer (B and C). Third, decide what tools and resources (D) you'll need to achieve this goal (e.g., people, coaching, training, money). Fourth, articulate the process—the steps—for getting there (E). This plan, as with other successful working plans, is meant to be *flexible*; you'll make changes as you proceed.

A. **My goal is** to clarify what I want to do next toward finding another position within my company.

B. **The benefits to me will be** refocused energy and feeling happier about my work.

C. **The benefits to my company and customers will be** increased productivity and commitment to customer needs.

D. **The tools and resources I'll need to fulfill this goal are as follows:**

▤ Skills inventory	▤ Career coaching sessions
▤ Networking with colleagues	▤ Values inventory
▤ Discussions with boss	▤ Reading professional articles

E. **These are the steps I'll take, although they may change as I proceed:**

1. Meet with career coach	**When**	Tuesday, April 5, 19__
2. Take inventories	**When**	Wednesday, April 13, 19__
3. Discuss plans with boss	**When**	Friday, April 15, 19__
4. Network for options	**When**	One interview a week for one month
5. Continue career coaching	**When**	One session a week for one month
6. Update my spouse about progress	**When**	During breakfast on Saturdays

Organizational Commitment to Worker Satisfaction

Kyle, a vice-president of research and development at a large computer manufacturer, is embarking on a mission to "increase worker satisfaction" in his division. "We have no choice," he said, "but to increase worker morale if we want to survive and compete." The research and development team has been working toward the goal of reducing product development cycle time from two or three years to eight or nine months. Achieving and sustaining this goal take continued diligence and expertise. As a result, the expert senior workers are getting pressured to perform, thus leaving little opportunity for the less advanced workers, or so-called junior workers, to advance or participate. Since the goal has been to reduce cycle time and manufacture quality products, the company can't afford to spend time and money on training workers.

From a career perspective, therefore, the senior workers are at the top of the ladder, doing the work, running the show, and feeling confined in a "performance box." The message to them is simply "Do your job, stick it out." They have a position and a paycheck. And junior workers have been stymied in their career. They have been discouraged from experimenting and learning, and they no longer have a ladder to climb. They are thinking, "If I can't move up, I'll move out." And some have moved out of the company. This organization, like most competitive organizations, cannot afford to lose budding talent.

Yet the workers at this firm *have* increased productivity, and their compensation levels are competitive. But to the company's chagrin, and despite a difficult job market, talented workers are still leaving. Job motivation and satisfaction cannot be guaranteed by offering higher salaries or promotions. Such resources have been stripmined. It is the responsibility of all workers to pay more attention to the less tangible, more elusive factors that add up to worker satisfaction.

The Families and Work Institute conducted a privately funded National Study of the Changing Workforce in which a sample of 2,958 wage and salary workers were interviewed. When workers were asked "What does success mean to you?" the response "Making a good income" ranked fourth out of six choices.[3] As Kyle learned, competitive salary levels are rarely enough to keep workers; eventually, they will leave to seek a workplace that offers personal satisfaction, recognition from others, *and* a good income.

A study done by Kyle's task force showed that one of the key reasons for "worker dissatisfaction" was the "lack of career options and development." As a result, the organization embarked on a career *self-management* program.

Its three primary objectives were as follows:

1. To educate staff in the area of career self-management in order to help empower all staff members to take responsibility for their own career mobility and job productivity.

2. To guide staff in the use of specific career tools for the purpose of enhancing their self-confidence and developing a deeper partnership between their individual needs and the organization's goals.

3. To coach and support staff to take specific career initiatives that would result in increased work satisfaction and productivity.

This program was introduced as a learning partnership between the company and the staff for *optimizing* individual career success and productivity. It was *not* a placement or outplacement program.

⊠

**Eileen Foreman, Bell Atlantic's manager
of management education, says, "We want to encourage
people to challenge assumptions, to be critical thinkers,
and to break the rules."**

*—Lori Bongiorno, "Corporate America's
New Lesson Plan," Business Week*

Global Joining

The key is for everybody to *make* a contribution and to *want* to move in the same direction. Penny Barrows, global career and business consultant, and Marsha Selva are planning to cosponsor ongoing conferences entitled "Vietnam: Addressing the Business Challenges." These conferences will be an outgrowth of a joint trip to Vietnam. Multinational experts will come together, each with a unique contribution to offer, each with a vision to open new frontiers between businesspeople in Vietnam and in the United States. Every expert will offer his or her services without financial remuneration. Each is passionate and committed to the venture. Financial payback will come later.

"Joining, for this group," Penny said, "represents an alignment of energy. I am the orchestra conductor who assembled the players; they are playing their own instruments and working out their programs together. For example, I formed a team of experts with different perspectives in similar fields. I'm asking them to stretch their thinking and create programs that incorporate their unique perspectives."

After each conference, the participants will resume their business practices, add one another to their network, and gain a new worldview.

The Personal Side of Joining:
Developing Self-Intimacy

Workers feel deeply when they must change, whether by choice or by force. Their feelings, however, are not always readily apparent. They continue to do their weekly grocery shopping, buy the Sunday newspaper, do household chores, and take their children to extracurricular activities. When asked, "How ya doing?" they frequently and spontaneously respond, "Well" or "OK."

With all the changes in workers' lives, how can things *appear* so normal? In my practice, I get paid to listen. When I'm not at work, I'm prone to listen too; it's a habit. People's feelings, I've discovered, are readily present. *Listen.* I stopped at the florist's recently, and as I paid for my purchase, the florist asked, "How are things?" I responded, "I'm very busy with my writing and practice. Thank you for asking." She appeared to be sad and quietly said, "You're lucky." She told me her business was slow and exhausting. I work with several clients who are well dressed and carry impressive titles. They begin to explore their career and life issues in a controlled manner. Unexpectedly, many start to weep as they describe their struggles at work or their efforts to find desirable work. Often they apologize for crying, embarrassed by displaying their emotion. Charles sniffled, "This is stupid. What am I crying about? I'm a man. I shouldn't be so emotional." Charles and others like him have a *tremendous* need to express their emotions—to take off the mask, to see and be seen beyond their clothing and title, to be heard, to be understood, to be accepted, and to be out of control and regain control. Charles needed to awaken his passion; he needed to be genuine. "At work, there is a spiritual dryness," Charles said. "We cannot go on simply making one *rational* decision after another. The reality is that, when management embarks on a change, people's emotions—

their spirit, how they feel about things—need to be considered as part of the reality—the change process."

You might be asking, "What do my feelings have to do with a 'self-employed' attitude and joining?" Feelings are our power. My passion drove me to collaborate with others to write this book. I sat in silence as Charles cried. He needed to feel his sadness, his anger, his hurt, or whatever he was feeling, in that moment. This was his truth—his authenticity, his integrity, his power—what he was missing at work.

Feeling in the moment is difficult for most of us but necessary in order to overcome fear and to express who we are. To be forced out—laid off or demoted—triggers feelings of betrayal, anger, hurt, and sometimes relief; to *choose* to make a change in your career—from working as an estate planner to being a management consultant, or quitting the law profession to become a fundraiser, for example—can evoke feelings of both excitement and fear. Survival and achieving success in our work lives by negotiating an uncertain and unpredictable marketplace are an emotional process. To ignore your feelings is to ignore your power. If I didn't have strong feelings about the subject I am writing about, I would not have the fortitude to write this book and build my practice. Emotional grappling—wrestling with your feelings and pinning them down—is also necessary to achieve independence and interdependence. If you don't grapple with your feelings, you might forever remain dependent on and controlled by what others feel and expect. Self-examination can be painful, but the payoffs are liberating.

Joining requires at least as much emotional, internal realignment as it does external, pragmatic action. Virginia had been a life insurance agent for eleven years. During that time, she had worked at a prestigious, world-renowned company and felt and acted as though she was "self-employed." She was enjoying an excellent income from commissions and repeat business. In Virginia's words, "Despite the time I had put in, the money I was earning, and the relationships I had built with my clients, something was missing. It all came to a head when a huge case reversed on me. I thought the deal was a sure bet, but at the last minute my client signed with another plan. Although I had had other case reversals, this one sent me into a depression. I was overwhelmed by my feelings, as though I was drowning."

Virginia talked to me about her anger toward her client and the disappointment she felt at losing the business. Still, she said, "My old value system is coming back to haunt me. My heart is no longer into convincing people to shelter their millions from Uncle Sam." She wanted to explore work that was more congruent with her values, but she also felt torn: She was finally earning a decent income and had built a substantial clientele. "At this point," she remarked, "I feel as if my business is controlling me. I'm not happy doing what I'm doing, but I'm making a good living. It's frightening to start all over again . . . new business, new clients, learning curve, and all that." At forty-five, it was frightening for Virginia to project ahead fifteen years to when she would be sixty. She did not want at sixty to say, "What I've done for most of my life isn't really what I wanted to be doing. I missed my calling." Virginia discovered that "joining herself" required *self-intimacy*: an effective way to answer the question, "What do I want to accomplish?"

What Do I Want to Accomplish?

A colleague, Mark Rosen, is a business manager and senior consultant at Interaction Associates, a management consulting firm. He frequently asks his executive clients, "What do you want to accomplish?" He feels this question grounds the clients and gets to the heart of their concerns. Mark doesn't want to waste their time or money. His clients typically respond by talking about what they want to change and what their goals are. Together, Mark and these clients start to think and focus in concrete terms. Mark then assesses whether his firm can provide the necessary expertise to help the clients achieve their goals.

At one point, I asked Virginia, "What do you want to accomplish?" At first she told me what she *no longer* considered an accomplishment. Virginia lamented, "I don't want to sell my soul for money. I don't want to live with this gnawing fear that if I change what I'm doing, I'll end up impoverished. I don't want to be poor, but I don't want to look back fifteen or twenty years from now and say I was afraid . . . afraid to do something different. I've attained a reasonable amount of financial independence, but money alone isn't enough." Virginia was clearly afraid that if she left her current situation, she might not succeed. She had accomplished some of her goals but yearned for something more. We went back to the question, "What do you want to accomplish?" "When I look down the road," she answered, "earning money is important, but making a contribution to people's lives is also important. In my work as a life insurance agent, the contribution part just isn't there. I want to make a contribution that I can feel proud of." Virginia, of course, feared the loss of her financial stability if she switched professions. She began to see that she was prejudging the marketplace and herself, speculating that there would be few opportunities in other fields for someone with her experience and abilities. I asked Virginia if she would try trading her judgment for curiosity, just temporarily. She agreed. Although her ideas were still vague, she was beginning the process of developing self-intimacy. I told her, as I do many of my clients, "There is honor in all work."

Some of my clients know immediately what they want to accomplish; they bring a statement of their goal to our first meeting. They seek my guidance in developing a plan and some practical suggestions for overcoming obstacles and supporting their dreams. Other clients are confused about their direction; they are unsure about what they want and what they bring to the workplace. I provide for them a safe, nonjudging environment, where they can talk about their fears, identify and understand their attributes, build confidence, and release their creativity to imagine what they would like to accomplish.

Curiosity First, Judgment Later

Whether people are *choosing* to make a change (in Virginia's case, a career change) or are being *forced* to make a change, many are quick to judge what they can and can't do. At the beginning phases of making a change, it is easy to see why people would want to hold on to what they know: Doing so is safe. Their judgment may be based on what they have learned in a recent performance review, through mass-media information and/or their survey of the *Occupational Outlook Handbook*, or from what I call "self-imposed fear." Ultimately, these judgments are all limiting. I guide my clients to both acknowledge and envision their lives *beyond* their current knowledge and feelings *and* to suspend judgment and adopt curiosity. I recommend that they gather information from multiple sources before coming to *any* conclusion.

Suspending judgment and adopting curiosity—questioning, researching, exploring—take courage. Johanna, an anthropologist and professor, remarked, "My associates know I'm making a career change, and they keep asking, 'What are you doing?' and 'What are you going to do?' They are uncomfortable with my answer; it is vague. I'm not ready to judge or put closure on my process. For once in my life, I need to sit back, observe myself and the world. To charge forward as if I'm going for another Ph.D. at this point would be counterproductive.

Instead, it's like I'm on an archaeological dig. I'm exploring. Who knows what I'll find?"

Johanna's curiosity, which is not linked to a specific goal, goes against many people's values and experience. Johanna's colleagues were uncomfortable with the degree of uncertainty in her life. Such people want answers: "I earn $50,000." "I'm a forest ecologist." "I'm a vice-president at Exxon." "I'm laid-off." "I'm interviewing at two companies." If you must give an answer, say, "I'm exploring. Do you mind if I ask *you* a question?" As Virginia, the insurance agent, discovered, it was her *questions* that led to her answers. A "self-employed" attitude requires curiosity—a means to extend your personal and professional boundaries and update your career or business choices. Note the difference between the curious and judging statements in the following examples. If you think of more comparative statements, write them down.

> *Curious:* I wonder why zebras have stripes?
> *Judging:* I don't like the zebra's stripes.
>
> *Curious:* I wonder what makes those people successful?
> *Judging:* They were probably born with a silver spoon in their mouth.
>
> *Curious:* Could you suggest career options that reflect my skills?
> *Judging:* I know all about what is out there.

Virginia's curiosity broadened her horizons. She asked her clients why they bought insurance from her, and they answered, "We trust you and you are knowledgeable." When I asked her what she liked best about her current work, she said, "Building relationships, influencing, advising, and helping others." Then she began to tell others what she liked doing best and asked them to suggest career possibilities. Virginia was overwhelmed with suggestions—teacher, part-time business lecturer, counselor, management consultant, account representative for a management consulting firm, fundraiser, innkeeper. On the surface, all of these jobs sounded foreign to Virginia, but as she examined each, she discovered common characteristics. In fact, most of these options would require her abilities in the areas of "building relationships, influencing, advising, and helping others." Virginia deliberated and networked with people who worked in some of the areas mentioned above. At first she chose to explore the field of management consulting. Then she looked more deeply into being an account representative for a management consultancy. The prospective career seemed to meet her two top criteria: She could make a difference in people's lives, and she could receive the salary she wanted. Virginia became convinced that her past work and her newly identified skills were directly applicable to the field. She attended association meetings, read trade journals, and networked. Ultimately, after a seven-month search, she identified consulting firms with different sizes, philosophies, and hiring criteria and accepted a position as an account representative at one of them.

Mentoring: When You Haven't Done It Before

Early in my business career, I had a mentor—someone who believed in me when I wasn't quite sure what I believed; someone who knew I had the basic skill and aptitude to do the job; and someone who was intrigued by the ways that I experimented, took risks, and eventually succeeded. This mentoring—joining—experience was *the* most significant catalyst in my business career. My mentor supported my curiosity; he encouraged the gestation of my belief that I could run a profitable business using my integrity, a core part of my power.

Returning once again to the case of Virginia, she found that the management consulting firm where she now worked offered products and services that, for example, would help salespeople learn to listen more effectively, managers to coach and not judge, line workers to make products that were error-free, leaders to turn vision into reality, and every worker to initiate solutions for problems. At her new job, Virginia met Harold, the president of the firm, who became her mentor. Harold appreciated her experience and values. He said, "I know you have not done this job before, but you can do it."

Harold mentored Virginia by reassuring her that she would have a generous period of time—four to six months—to learn the business, including product and service knowledge and the firm's team approach, and to develop major accounts. He maintained an open-door policy with all workers and suggested that Virginia meet with him twice a week to discuss what she was learning and how to overcome any obstacles she encountered. Specifically, when Virginia asked a question, Harold would respond, "What do *you* think?" In addition, Harold reminded Virginia that he respected *her* expertise, opinions, and unique style; they were refreshing and valuable to the firm and its clientele. Basically, he fostered an independent and interdependent relationship.

If we all had a mentor like Harold at some point in our careers, we would undoubtedly progress beyond our expectations and in return support others. Mentoring does not have to be restricted to a relationship with only one other person. People can carefully choose to join *teams* and *organizations* and find that the community or group can be a mentor. These teams and organizations provide support, direction, and opportunities for growth and contribution; they possess values, mission statements, stimulating projects, and rewards.

[Productivity is] not magic; it's getting people to a point where they can empower themselves.

—Stan Evans, vice-president of sales and marketing,
Blackwell Scientific Publications, Inc.

Peer Work Requires Inner Work: Clarify Your Values

Coming to terms with your value system is essential when making business decisions, evaluating your ideas, accepting projects, seeking full-time work, and collaborating with a team. Clarifying your values is part of the necessary inner work for developing a "self-employed" attitude. Your values are not set in stone. If they were, individual change would be impossible. The inner work helps you to recognize what your present values are, thus enhancing your self-esteem and spurring you to action.

As you clarify and prioritize your values, you will make positive choices. Virginia did this as she searched for worthwhile work. She made it a point in her exploratory discussions with colleagues to say, "It's a priority that I work with a management consulting firm that is socially conscious. It's not enough just to increase profits." As she networked and interviewed, she was guided by this value and listened for information that would help her to make an educated choice.

Doing your inner work fuels your outer mobility too. Without your inner work, you would be unable to share what you believe or to apply your own personal standards to make critical decisions. If one of your values is "doing work that benefits people," then you won't pursue work that doesn't meet that criterion. Sometimes, naturally, you will be enticed by other possibilities (e.g., money, travel, leading others, a title). When your core values are compromised, however, you may well end up with a job or new project but eventually will be unhappy with your choice.

Gail, a school superintendent, said, "My passion can be viewed as the intersection of philosophy, psychology, and business. Philosophically, I believe in doing work that makes people's lives better. Psychology comes into play in understanding why people do what they do.

Business involves influencing people. I am at my best when I use all three in my work." Gail makes difficult choices. Practically, she looks at the facts before she makes a decision; there is too much at stake otherwise. She uses her passion to help her make decisions. Determination, using "will" alone, can, after a protracted period of time, lead to drudgery and frustration.

When you look inside, your inner work will *never* be wasted. It gives life and shape to your vision, whatever the outcome. I want you to hear—embrace—these words: As you and the world continue to change, the inner work is your only real security. The fruits of this work are in experiencing the commitment and energy to express and realize your goals and to serve others.

An "In" and an "Out"

The concept of joining emphasizes flexibility, not complacency or rigidity. By this time, you know the maxim "You must know and be loyal to yourself." The contract "employer and employee dependence" has been rewritten. Under the new terms, all workers need an "in" and an "out" as a means to ensure their success and survival. In your mind, for example, commit fully to a three-month project (in), but be prepared to renegotiate your situation or to leave (out) if the joining process does not prove mutually beneficial. David, a former architect, opened a fast-food franchise. He bought in and also developed an alternative plan (out) in the event that running the franchise didn't meet his expectations. David later decided to sell the franchise, because the eighty-hour-per-week schedule required to run a successful operation did not allow enough time for other obligations in his life. The franchisor bought the franchise back. Sally, a senior technician, was laid off by one division in her company; soon after, she was offered another position in a different division. Although relieved by the offer, she made a six-month commitment—to herself—in which she would do her work (in) and prepare for leaving (out) if her arrangement proved unsatisfying. To create an "in" and an "out," be prepared—develop a financial cushion, and know your skills, abilities, aptitudes, and the marketplace.

The peer-work bond is creating and doing work from which both parties benefit.

Joining . . .

without obligation.
with purpose.

without fear.
with passion.

without dependence.
with independence and interdependence.

without signed contracts.
with personal commitment.

without drudgery.
with authenticity, collaboration, and productivity.

COMMITTING TO
CONTINUOUS LEARNING

View your career as a lifetime endeavor

EMPLOYED ATTITUDE

Dependent Mindset

I can hold on to my successes and be satisfied. If I can only get what I want—position, title, benefits—then I can rest on my past accomplishments.

SELF-EMPLOYED ATTITUDE

Independent and Interdependent Mindset

I will commit to continuous learning, personal growth, and gaining new perspectives. My career is a lifetime endeavor. My mistakes and successes lead to expanded thinking and further contribution.

MANY OF YOU IN AND OUTSIDE ORGANIZATIONS TODAY ARE ANXIOUS—you feel as though something is about to drop down on you from above. You might worry about being laid off, fired, or demoted. Or you might be bored to death, doing the same old thing. But you console yourself by saying, "At least I'm getting paid. Compared with the next guy, I'm doing pretty well." But *are* you? *Do you feel you are learning something new each day?*

In the work world of the 1990s, no one's job is guaranteed. I've said this before; the importance of saying it again is that you *hear* it, for that is the first step toward action. The time has come for you to listen and refocus, to learn to harness your internal resources. Simply working hard at your job will not protect you from the layoffs, buyouts, mergers, and restructuring so prevalent in today's organizations. Successful people are working two jobs. A job description for one of these, career self-manager, appears in the Introduction, and the second is the position such people currently hold.

◪

I need to be learning from and challenged by what I'm doing. My life's work is beyond any one organization. . . . I'm constantly learning, no matter where I am.

—*John Haskell, organizational development consultant*

Today, successful people are working two jobs.

Your role as an individual is . . . taking responsibility for your own career growth and job productivity while making a contribution to the organization and your customers. Responsibility includes taking the initiative in your career planning, negotiating with management for self-development needs, and recognizing ways in which you can add value to the organization.

The organization's role is . . . joining workers at all levels to support "career self-management" practices. Joining includes career guidance, recognition for experimentation and job performance, and encouragement for ongoing personal and professional learning.

Seeing Your Life and Learning from It

You've most likely heard someone say, "There is a book inside everyone." I believe this to be true. Everybody's lifetime—her or his journey—is a series of events and stories that can be configured into chapters with a central theme. Sit down and think about the *texture* of your life. I believe each of you will see and reexperience vibrant colors, intriguing scenes, loving and painful episodes, mysterious and uncertain times, unanswered questions, stimulating and uneventful conversations, unexpected disarray, and peak productivity. Few of us choose to write autobiographically. Some of us attempt to while others follow through by keeping a journal; some of us read *about* others, finding satisfaction therein; and some of us aspire to a day when we might put pen to paper.

In this chapter, I encourage you to *see* your career life and *learn* from it, to *understand* and *explain* what you've seen and experienced. Through talking and writing about your experiences, you'll gain a deeper understanding and *own*—take pride in—your abilities and uniqueness. This is a lifetime process; be patient, persistent, and tolerant, and learn from your and others' mistakes and successes. Be prepared—take notes along the way.

Too often, we are blinded by "doing" and are actually unable to see what we do. We dig a joyless rut, live an unexamined career life, as though someone else or something else were in control. It's a struggle to sit still and reevaluate yourself, especially when you've been rewarded for "doing." Sophia, a finance account executive, said to me, "In another life, I'd be a costume designer." "Sophia," I asked, "what about in *this* life?" While *you* may never write your autobiography, do think about deepening your understanding of who you are, why you do what you do, and what you bring to the world; this is your security. Do "tell your stories." Your stories are vignettes, each containing a beginning, a middle, and an end; they bring your history to life for yourself and others and illustrate how your life story can apply to your desires and to customers' needs.

Here is an example of a brief story written by Vivian, an unchallenged human resource manager, describing why she left the company where she had worked for three years. Vivian wrote this story both to clarify for herself why she left and to create a tool for succinctly presenting her decision to potential employers.

I chose to join this company because it offered me an opportunity to expand my ideas and build a top-notch human resources organization in a team-oriented atmosphere. After two years, I discovered that I was unable to implement change, due to conflicting leadership styles among us. I realized that my priorities were to make decisions and to influence the organization's direction. However, I continued to feel blocked and frustrated in my work, and I left—on good terms.

Next I joined a management consulting practice but, after a year, found that I missed dealing directly with internal organizational issues.

Now I am seeking a position where I can influence people personally and can successfully design and implement human resource policies and programs that are flexible and tailored to meet diverse worker needs and organizational goals.

In my grandfather's day, people would sit for long hours telling one another stories about the Old Country and the New. If they ran out of stories, they listened to the radio. Storytelling was an expression of the texture and fiber of their lives—work, family, and social endeavors. Storytelling helped them to understand their times, share what they did, and appreciate one another.

To begin telling *your* stories, I encourage each of you to identify positive life or work experiences, one or two from childhood and adolescence, and three or four from adulthood. Here are five questions that you might ask yourself:

1. What challenge did I face and what did I do to solve the problem?

2. What skills and personal qualities did I demonstrate in meeting this challenge?

3. What was the outcome?

4. What did I enjoy about the experience; how did I benefit?

5. How did I benefit others by solving this problem?

Rather than telling *and* writing your own story, ask a friend to write down your story as you describe your experiences. After you are through telling your story, ask your friend to read what you have said. Another option is to tape-record your story, then play it back. Whichever option you choose, listen to your story; it is filled with valuable information about what you enjoy, what you do well, and how you do what you do. This information will help you better to see and experience yourself. It is vital for your security—your personal growth and career mobility.

Before attempting to tell and write their stories, many of my clients say, "I've contacted fifty people, but nothing is happening," "I'm not sure what to do next," or "I've done lots of things, but so what?" I often respond by asking, "Do you know what you want *now*? Do you know what you bring to today's workplace?" I explain that if they don't know the answers to these questions, then they'll be wasting their energies and creating needless frustration for themselves. One of my clients, Kerry, a news commentator and radio talk-show host, said, "I'm having trouble putting together a résumé. I'm confused and unfocused; I have too much information to sort through." I asked him, "Can you name three skills—only three—that you *want* to bring into the marketplace?" He looked relieved; my question provided focus, and he named three skills. Subsequently, he shared with me several stories about his accomplishments. These stories reinforced and supported his skills, providing information that we organized into his résumé.

You Can Commit to Continuous Learning

Compare the items in the two columns below and note the characteristics that best describe your commitment to learning.

Hold on to the Past	*Engage in Continuous Learning*
Deny that things have changed; believe that others need to change but not you.	Notice how you and the environment are changing; believe that you can learn how, regardless of your age.
Ignore your feelings about change; spend your energies squelching your anxiety.	Talk with others about how you're feeling about personal change and the changes around you.
Defend what you do and how you do it as the best or only way.	Stay open to the possibility that you can learn new methods, improve your performance, and increase your productivity.
Depend on others to manage your career.	Become a career self-manager; initiate and plan your learning.
Stay confined to your title.	Rewrite your job description or your career goal and propose a new title.
Try to do only what you want to do.	Examine what you want and how it is relevant to the needs of others.

Glued to Your Title?

Kerry wanted a different challenge. His title—news commentator and radio talk-show host—no longer reflected who he was and what he wanted to do. He had a new goal: to work with a national television station as a news reporter and commentator. Your title—employment manager, programmer, vice-president of finance—may also represent a confining box. In another era your title worked; at present, however, it may not be serving you or the marketplace. Your title is only a temporary creation, designed as an appendage for meeting ego, organizational, and customers' needs. What's behind your title? What do you *now* bring and what do you *want* to bring to your customers? That's what we all need to know and what our customers will buy. Every successful self-employed person knows this.

Job titles, along with jobs, are being eliminated. Caught in the middle of most large organizations, for example, the "manager of" is a victim of the trend toward advanced information systems and flatter organizational structures. As a result, many have reshaped their careers and retitled themselves. Kerry did the same; he traded "holding on to the past" for "continuous learning" and considered the tradeoffs shown on the previous page.

Letting go of your title and creating another are often a confusing and painful process. Kerry expressed many people's sentiment: "I have this panicky feeling, as though I have nothing to hold on to." Laboring under this ambiguity, doing your current job and/or looking for another job, even if you are voluntarily making a change, and understanding that "you are *not* your title" are challenges for anybody. Kerry reminded himself continuously, "I am in transition; I'll be OK. Letting go of my title isn't easy, but it is a positive step toward my goal." So often, at work, at a party, at lunch, at the grocery store, or at home, people ask us, "What do you do?" Frequently we respond with our *title*, "I am a . . ." Doing so is convenient and safe. It has been my experience that if I choose, in lieu of my title, to explain what I *do* (which is much more accurate and meaningful than my title), most people tend not to listen. Their eyes glaze over, as if "the process" I engage in is too difficult or takes too much work to comprehend.

Confusion and pain, as Kerry discovered, seem to rise as ambiguity—lack of focus—increases. Ambiguity is a clue, a message to go through a process of self-assessment, part of which requires "burning the grass": being alone, asking questions, not having immediate answers, and assimilating new ideas. Our forebears and my grandfather did; you can too. Others want answers, and we are conditioned to give them. Our challenge is to share our present truth, to overcome our fear even if we are uncertain about what we want. Tell people, for example, "I'm in transition. What I was doing no longer met my needs; therefore, I am taking this time to assess what I want." If they don't understand in the moment, go on; possibly, someday they will.

I'm beginning to learn and respect that what I'm doing today is likely to change tomorrow. Hiding behind the safety of my title masks my growth. What I have to give to people is my "learning about what I know." I can't learn and give what I know if I confine myself to a title—a box; it is limiting. Another solution I have found is to begin the conversation with a title, for example, career consultant, and follow with a descriptive phrase: "I'd like to describe what I do. I coach individuals in and outside of organizations to assess themselves, redirect their careers, and increase their productivity." In this way, I am satisfying them and me. I can change my description as I evolve and the market changes; moreover, down the road, if I need to, I can also change my title.

I remind myself and coach my clients, "Your spouse will still love you, your friends will still invite you to play golf, your children will continue to enjoy playing with you, and you can be as creative and resourceful as you want to be whether you are a lawyer, professor, chef, or vice-president. You are not alone in your struggle out of the box. The struggle is a necessary part of your growth." To stay glued to your title can be a resignation to your past or a denial of your current work situation. Learning—living—doesn't happen within the boundaries of our titles, a place where our fears can fester; rather, it occurs in stretching and reconfiguring what we have created or has been created for us.

I heard on WBUR public radio, in Boston, that we—the public—allow famous people to "labor under ambiguity." We think it's OK for people like Hillary Rodham Clinton and Ted Turner to grow and develop, make their mistakes, redefine themselves, *and* contribute, all at once. We look up to and need to idolize them; they are different—special. We can learn from them. My suspicion is that many public figures wrestle with ambiguity. They, I imagine, give themselves permission to persevere and overcome the obstacles that may be blocking their greater purpose. I encourage and support my clients to do the same. Not only can they be derailed by the judgment of others, but as their internal tape plays, many judge themselves. Letting go of your title is not a mechanical process but an emotional one. It takes time, patience, flexibility, and skill, especially when you've been forced to give it up.

Angles Arrien, a crosscultural anthropologist, identified five universal symbols: the triangle, the circle, the square, the spiral, and the equidistant cross. She says, "Symbols are the universal language. They bridge the invisible worlds with the visible worlds. The decades of the 1990s and going into 2000 will be a time of learning how to walk the mystical [independent and interdependent] path with practical feet, how to have a leg in both worlds, the inner and the outer."[1] Many of us in the 1980s lived in the square (the box)—the symbol for stability and security—within our niche or title. Many of us also got stuck there.

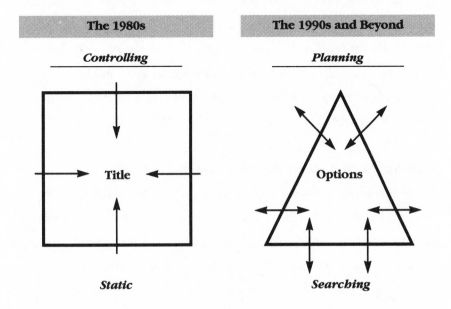

If you are forced out of or choose to abandon your title, you will live in the square less and live in the triangle—the symbol for the planner and the searcher—more, identifying your skills and values and matching them with customers' needs. You'll need to be able to describe what you do—for example, research, present, write, diagnose—for this is what employers and customers will buy, not your title. The following "action-results statement" illustrates this point:

I wrote (action verb) an article for Fortune *magazine about collaboration in the workplace, and it resulted in my receiving an invitation from a division vice-president to submit a proposal to do team building for a group of senior executives.*

This is an active statement that presents what you *do* or *did*, as opposed to presenting your title, "I'm a project manager." Your title, represented by the square, won't suffice anymore. In the following pages, you'll find (1) the definition of an action-results statement, (2) a guide to writing your own such statement, and (3) examples of action-results statements. Whether you work in a company full- or part-time, own your own business, or are looking for your first job, action-results statements can help you articulate your talents, skills, and experiences as a means of expressing who you are, what you have done, and how you can add value to an organization or a customer.

Examples of Action-Results Statements

These statements were written by individuals working in a variety of professions and actively involved in enhancing their current job or seeking a different job. Note that each statement is composed of three parts: (1) an action word, (2) a description of what was done and for whom, and (3) the outcome or results.

▤ **Coached** sales representatives and managers on specific sales situations, including overcoming buyer resistance and cold-call rejection, resulting in advancing selling skills, retaining clients, and increasing business.
  —*Business consultant*

▤ **Designed and communicated** corporate benefits package, including payroll-based, executive, work and family, and international benefit plans, leading to current packages that meet worker/employer needs.
  —*Director, benefits planning*

The Action-Results Statement: A Definition

An action-results statement is clear and concise. Its purpose is to help you clarify and understand your capabilities and be able to articulate them to others. For your job productivity and career mobility, the statement can be organized into tools, such as a "capabilities and accomplishments statement," a marketing letter, or a personal biography. An action-results statement has three parts:

1. It begins with an action word or verb. This word represents one of your skills, such as *presented*.

2. It next describes what you did and for whom, such as *a core middle-management training program that highlighted team building and leadership development.*

3. It then states outcomes or results, such as *resulting in 95 percent participation and the delivery of the same program to other managers.*

Putting these three parts together completes the statement:

Action-Results Statement: Presented a core middle-management training program that highlighted team building and leadership development, resulting in 95 percent participation and the delivery of the same program to other managers.

Try writing one action-results statement. Use the example provided above as a guideline. A simple way to identify your skills and their effectiveness is to tell a friend a story about one of your accomplishments and how you achieved it. Ask your friend to write down skills and action phrases as you tell your story. Use the skills and action phrases to begin writing other action-results statements.

≣ **Promoted** employee involvement as part of an overall quality
and productivity improvement strategy. As a result, more than
200 quality circles were established companywide.
—*Director, staff development*

≣ **Directed** the formation and execution of an expert system-
based problem diagnostic tool, resulting in a 55 percent
improvement in diagnostic time and cost.
—*Reliability manager*

A Case Example: Kerry

To make the transition from news commentator and radio talk-show
host to national television news reporter and commentator, Kerry
decided to construct his action-results statements differently. He turned
them around into *results-action statements*. In the media world, Kerry's
customers wanted to hear, quickly, what he had accomplished. "Sound
bites," Kerry explained, "is their program. To get my foot in the door, I
need to be able to speak their language. Presenting my accomplishments first and then following with the way I achieved them is a better
way to get their attention."

Here are examples of results-action statements Kerry presented in
his résumé and in conversation with potential employers:

≣ *Ratings increased by 25 percent during the last year* due to the
unusual guests I recruited for my show, the timing of the show,
and my interviewing style.

≣ *Awarded several commendations from the president of the
station* for timely reporting and in-depth interviewing.

≣ *Received a personal letter from a foreign world leader* for
"gracefully and tactfully handling delicate issues" in a recent
interview with him.

The Struggle to Move from the Box to the Triangle

Analyzing what you do, writing about what you do, letting go of the parts of your work that you've grown beyond, and then deciding what you want to market can be extremely frustrating. It is rarely without resistance that people put aside their title and go about the process of analyzing and writing about what they do.

This transition from a work title that is no longer representative of what one does or wants to do is demonstrated in the case of Martin, a "programmer." Previously Martin spent little time at the computer; now he is called on by division managers to consult with them on technical problems. Martin's programming job has evolved into technical consulting, and his title has changed accordingly, from programmer to technical consultant.

Although this "consultant" felt passionate about his new role, he still disliked his job. As we analyzed the situation together, he discovered that it was not the job he disliked but the lack of recognition he received in his consulting role. "Programmer" no longer fit; "technical consultant" did. Following the principle that "we are all self-employed," Martin took control of his career. First, he wrote ten action-results statements to document what he actually did for work. Martin chose the action-results format because his priority as a consultant was how he did his job. We then role-played so that he became familiar with talking about his new role. Soon after, he initiated a conversation with his boss, during which Martin elaborated on his new role, pointing to its virtues both to the organization and to himself, and talked about how his current job title was a misrepresentation of his "consultant" status. Martin now saw himself differently, and his boss began to see him in a different light—as "technical consultant," a fitting title, at least for now.

Work and career are perpetual discovery.
This is a question not only of individual initiative . . .
The organization must not see people as positions,
but [as] people who can move in all kinds of directions
and play different roles. Movement cannot be seen as demotion.
Organizations need to encourage people to get in touch
with what they want to do.

—John Shibley, director of training and development, L. L. Bean

Many of my clients say, "It's lonely." Some report, "It's boring when I analyze myself, but I'm good at helping others do so." Others admit, "I'm afraid of discovering that I won't have much to offer out of the context of my current work." And many exclaim, "Why can't I sell my title and the list of my skills? I've always found work that way before!"

If you are looking for just "a job"—a put-food-on-the-table type of job—then selling your title and a list of your skills *may* work. But if you want more, to uncover your authentic self and live your passion, then telling your story and examining what you do and how you do it are essential. Three obstacles frequently arise for my clients during the transitional process: fear of change, *despite* their stated desire for change; lack of knowledge about the current realities of the workplace; and impatience with themselves and/or others.

Risk

Risk is critical to developing and managing your career. To encourage people to become risk takers, Colleen Clark, vice-president of human resources at Eastern Mountain Sports, says, "I constantly ask people what they learned from this or that experience. I encourage people not to judge based on one short-term interaction but to learn from it and incorporate their action into the larger scheme of things."

Learning has no end, but many beginnings. I often hear from people who are working, from those who have lost their jobs, and from those between jobs that they lack "focus" or "direction." Herein lie the learning for many and the willingness, as Robert Frost said, to be "lost enough to find yourself." You may be afraid to be lost, rightfully so, especially if you question your ability to find yourself, have had little practice in self-examination, or are impatient with your change process. This, I believe, is the case for most of us. We lack practice and patience, and/or deny what is natural: personal and world change. Every one of us has a choice: to *learn* that these realities deserve our respect and that we must learn from them or to play it safe—isolate ourselves, climb career ladders, and wait for opportunities to knock.

Few of us feel the permission to risk—although risk is a crucial element to our learning and success. Excuses will not work in today's demanding workplace, which leaves us with the responsibility for analyzing problems, confronting issues, and resolving them. It is time to view risk as a "learning runway," necessary for the takeoff toward new possibilities.

On the runway, there are no guarantees; you might take off or you might not. If you do take off, to where and to what height? If you don't, then what? Many of you are taking a risk by reading and thinking about and testing the notion that "we are all self-employed." You are learning—questioning, researching, experimenting, and evaluating—and are giving up some old ways of thinking and acting and adopting some new ways.

☒

**I'm responsible and accountable; this is fulfilling, exciting,
and terrifying. It can be a real roller coaster. I try to take the
long-term view; success and failure are part of the nature
of things. . . . Celebrate the successes, learn from the failures,
and move on.**

*—Tim McGovern, manager of software development,
Massachusetts Institute of Technology*

Using Paradox

Paradoxical statements can appear contradictory; paradoxes are. Yet such statements can also contain a truth about living authentically and productively. To my grandfather's neighbors, "burning the grass" seemed unproductive and chaotic. But to my grandfather, it represented growth—each season the grass grew back greener. The following stories demonstrate four paradoxes and how my clients used them in their attempts to forge new directions.

Paradox 1: Risk Is Safety

Priscilla, a software networks engineer, was fired from her job and soon after found a similar job in a small, fast-growing company. At first Karen, her new boss, collaborated with Priscilla by talking over plans and asking for her input before implementing them. But "after a few weeks," Priscilla said, "Karen's questions suddenly turned into demands. She would simply say, 'Get it done by Friday.' " Priscilla was afraid to lose her job again and tried to deny her hurt feelings about being excluded from the planning process. After another month, she admitted, "I have this insidious feeling that I might be fired again. Maybe I'm still feeling the trauma from the last time." I proposed that Priscilla take a risk and confront her fear by sharing her feelings with her boss.

When Priscilla met with Karen, she said, "I'm here because I value our relationship. When I started this job, I felt included in the planning process; you sought my opinions, and we were meeting our goals. In the past month, though, things have changed. I'm feeling excluded— I'm ordered to do things. Could we talk about the reasons for the change?" Rather than playing it safe, Priscilla took a risk. She shared her feelings and didn't make an accusation or demand. Karen told Priscilla about the pressure *she* was under as a new manager. Together, they talked about ways in which they could support each other.

Paradox 2: "Self-employment" Is Employability

In the past three years, Lois, a medical documentation project manager, has contributed significantly to increasing sales in the small consulting firm where she works. She not only developed manuals that satisfied clients' training and information needs but also managed project teams and developed several new accounts. Then Roger, the new vice-president of marketing, offered Lois a 10 percent raise and a revised contract. Roger wanted to partner with Lois in an all-out effort to expand the firm's client base.

Lois neither signed the contract nor accepted the raise. In her next meeting with me, however, she talked about how hard she had worked during the past three years and commented, "I'm angry that I've been given a 10 percent raise, which basically means I'm not being seen for my accomplishments and ability. In their eyes, I'm just an employee. I don't feel like an employee; I've helped the business to grow and I've brought in customers."

I responded, "Let's work at deepening your understanding of 'self-employment.' That will help you to increase your employability." I suggested that Lois think about the sentences "I'm my own employer. My company is my customer." This is the notion that Kirby Timmons, cited in chapter 4, espoused. Lois listened carefully, became curious, and asked, "How can I apply this idea to my situation?" Knowing about Lois's excellent performance record, her enthusiasm, and the firm's stage of growth, I suggested that she write her own contract and include in it an incentive plan modeled after those developed in other, more mature consulting firms. Lois exclaimed, "That's right! Roger is my customer, and I'm my own employer. I've been satisfying the firm's needs, and this is an opportunity to reestablish my relationship with a good customer."

When I last saw Lois, she had asked Roger for a three-week period to think about the contract and the incentive plan. She told me she was committed to her job and to researching the incentive compensation plans offered by other consulting businesses. Lois was planning to present her own proposal and incentive plan to Roger; these would include the results of her thorough research, documentation of her past achievements, and a concise outline of how she would contribute to the firm's expansion strategy. Lois remarked, "If I don't act on the notion that self-employment is employability, I'll probably be unhappy and less productive. Eventually, if I don't choose to leave . . . who knows? I'd likely get fired anyway."

Paradox 3: Winter Is a Time of Growth

It is winter as I write this. The earth appears bleak—snow-covered ground, bare trees, a cloudy sky. But I remind myself that underneath the snow, spring percolates—growth is coming—and I remind my clients too. The soil and trees are storing nutrients and preparing for warmth. Behind the clouds, the sun shines. A client of mine, Dennis, a state government administrator, left his job. "I needed to recharge, and work was not the place. I was in a rut and lost my enthusiasm," Dennis remarked. Although he had savings, he was out of work. To others, it looked like he was simply sitting around wasting his time. Dennis's friends and family had difficulty understanding and accepting his behavior. Dennis said, "My wife says, 'Get a job. You've been out of work for two months.' My response to her has been, 'I've been working nonstop for twenty-five years. I need to rethink things.'"

Dennis has been meeting with me for support and encouragement to use his "winter as a time of growth." Neither he nor I can always tell what is happening, but we both know it is a productive time. Dennis takes long walks, plays racquetball with his friends, enjoys being with his children, reads, and sometimes sits and does nothing. He is *not* depressed; he is *learning* from the winter. He is learning to say, "I'm using this time to think about my skills and interests, and the form my future takes is yet to be determined." Winter always leads to spring!

Paradox 4: Self-Awareness Is a Contribution to Others

"I feel it's selfish to spend this time learning about who I am," remarked Grace, a grants writer. Grace has earned two master's degrees and has worked for the past fifteen years in several part-time jobs—planner, management consultant, fundraiser, and field-work supervisor—while raising two children. Her children are more independent now, but saving for their college tuition is fast becoming a priority. Grace feels a personal need to fully apply her education and passion toward helping others. "My husband and family just want me to get a full-time job," Grace said. "But I don't seem to be able to do that. I'm at the stage in my life when I need to figure out what *I* really want. I feel guilty doing this. Also, over the years, I've lost some of my professional self-confidence. I'd be competing with some very talented people who have been dedicated to their work."

Grace's greatest competition is herself. In the past, she had always taken the first job she was offered. This time, although she vowed to plan and assess before she made any commitment, she needed my guidance to stay the course. I said to Grace, "You are talented, well educated, and multilingual, and you have superior communication skills. This is the time to give yourself permission to understand better how you want to harness your attributes and discover how they are relevant to the marketplace. Your self-awareness is your contribution to others *and* to yourself."

Grace has scheduled several informational interviews with former colleagues and associates to become reacquainted with them and the current work world. In these meetings, she will seek only information. One question she will ask is, "I am here because I trust your opinion. From your point of view, what do you believe are my three best assets?" After Grace meets with about seven of her contacts, a theme will begin to emerge about how others see her and how she might contribute to the world. Through their feedback, she will be better able to harness her skills and contribute to others.

At first glance, the four paradoxes explored above are often confusing. Yet as these case vignettes show, they represent some of the deepest, most difficult aspects of changing ourselves and our view of the world. The rewards of embracing a paradox usually far outweigh the cost.

Transition: The Bridge throughout History

Transition has always been a part of our organizational and individual evolution. We often don't see it, because we are in it. My grandfather, for example, somehow understood transitions—he would step back, then do what he thought was right. He knew that shades of black and gray camouflaged the positive aspects of transition, but he could also envision the rewards for moving through it. He lived through the recession of 1907, the depression of 1929, both world wars, and the Korean conflict. Through them, he struggled and eventually prospered.

Transition is a rite of passage: the process of growth from one form to another. Individually, for example, it is manifest in the changes from adolescence to adulthood or from single status to marriage; societally, from an agricultural to a manufacturing economy or from an autocratic state to a democratic government; or organizationally, from a fledgling start-up to a bustling midsize enterprise or from proprietary to open systems manufacturing.

Learning and Transition Guidelines

As you reframe your work and career, at times you will feel confused and anxious. These are inescapable characteristics of learning and transition. You won't always know all the answers; nor will you be expected to have all the answers. Here are some ways to help yourself:

- **Don't push.** Do participate. You'll learn as you think about your past, answer questions, hear from others, and plan for the future.

- **Don't panic.** This is an opportunity to figure out what you want and how you can be more productive in *or* outside your organization.

- **Expect discomfort.** Distress is a sign not that something has gone wrong but that something is changing. During any transition, it is common to feel anxious—to feel both threatened and excited by new possibilities. Exercising, talking with a trusted colleague or friend, and writing in a journal are some ways to manage stress and anxiety.

▤ **Allow for learning.** Your ability to risk and learn has brought
   you to this point. Continue—give yourself permission and time
   to learn new things.

▤ **Take care of yourself.** Do little things that make you feel
   good. Take walks, read, or watch your favorite TV programs.
   Don't force change—take breaks.

Respect Your Inner Voice

It's been a long haul for Anne, a nursing director. During most of her
work life, she has felt that she was compromising her true abilities. She
has worked *for* her bosses, never considering any other possibilities. At
her most recent job, her boss was a detail person; you know the type,
cross the "*t*'s" and dot the "*i*'s." Anne's personality is at the other end
of the spectrum; although she respects the need for detail, she is a big-
picture person—someone who creates a vision and takes action by
clearly defining the necessary steps and guiding and managing others
toward reaching the goal—in other words, a manager *and* a leader.

Anne's inner voice, buried under years of compromise, often whis-
pers to her, "I am a leader." When her boss left the medical institution
for another job, Anne took this event as a cue to seek a career consultation with me in order, in her words, "to listen to my inner voice, to
tell others, 'I am a leader.' " Anne's meetings with me were an opportunity for her to learn from her past. Her goals were to understand her
true abilities and learn how she could become her own best advocate
for doing work that more closely represented who she was and what
she had to contribute.

I asked Anne, "What would be the purpose of listening to your
inner voice?" Enthusiastically, she responded, "To become more familiar with my natural abilities; to name what they are. I want to strength-

en my conviction so that I can become a candidate for an internal position as vice-president of nursing . . . a leadership position." Anne spent several sessions discussing her past. She told me stories about her abilities in three central areas: leadership, management, and internal consulting. The following are brief examples of Anne's original stories:

Leadership

Generally, I believe my role is to develop staff and all other workers who are committed to care. One way that I followed through on this vision was to create and develop monthly educational seminars to help staff understand the chronic pain of cancer patients. I also encouraged one of the chief physicians, Alan, to join me in an effort to form a new position and establish funding for a half-time chronic pain expert. With his advocacy skills and my ability to sell the idea to different departments, including the chronic pain unit, we now have a part-time expert who aids patients and educates staff.

Management

I changed the staffing structure of an inpatient setting and reduced management positions from four to two. This was a good example of my ability to negotiate with staff and union members. I showed my concern for those who would be losing their jobs, and I put the facts on the table: We needed more direct primary care, not more management. After some debate, we substituted two managers for three primary-care staff.

Consultation

Through in-depth, face-to-face interviewing, I surveyed thirty professional staff members in eight different medical facilities to gather information about their ethical concerns and their interpretations of the patient's right to choose treatment. My staff and I compiled the data, and I presented the findings to the board of our facility.

In the process of telling her story, Anne explained, understood, and owned her abilities. Her voice deepened, her posture became more erect, and she smiled confidently. She developed a "self-employed" attitude, saying, "If I don't get the vice-president position, I'll be prepared to look elsewhere for a leadership position." Anne learned that at any point in her career, she could always respect the texture of her inner voice.

Gracefully Bold

Like Anne, if you've attended to your inner voice, your outer voice will change as a result. It will become more flexible and stronger, but not brash. Holly, a labor relations specialist, noted, "As I talk about what I've done, I'm developing the confidence to become 'gracefully bold.' I tell people what I can do and what I can't or don't want to do without beating them over the head with my accomplishments or my preferences."

I work as a team member with a client. I get a lot of information about what the clients need and like. Then I create a fine piece that is a blend of their input and my creative input. My clients know their business better than I do. I ask them to give me information, and I apply it to the creative process.

—Ed Halstead, graphic designer

To enhance your career or attract new customers, you will need to know yourself and be able to articulate how what you offer meets another's needs. Most professionals have never had to tell their stories or present themselves as service providers. In the past job market, their skills or products were accepted at face value—high-tech, real estate, finance. *Grace* is knowing yourself. To be *bold* is to express your authentic self in such a way that you are serving others and yourself. This is a new and difficult concept, but it is a crucial one for survival now and in the future.

Learning from and Reframing Your Mistakes

Developing a "self-employed" attitude is a process. As with most processes, this one requires that you learn from your mistakes. Thomas, an events coordinator and consultant at a nonprofit agency, worked *for* an authoritarian boss, Clark, who blamed others when anything went wrong and rarely respected the opinion of staff unless that opinion was closely aligned with his own. During Thomas's job interviews, Clark had said, "I encourage others to share their opinions" and "People get a lot of latitude around here for trying different ways of doing things." Thomas had accepted the position because he liked the job responsibilities and what Clark had said.

Within two weeks, Thomas reported, "I discovered that Clark did not 'walk his talk.' He berated staff who shared their own ideas, and although we had not had a confrontation yet, I became aware that my independent style would not jibe with his." Thomas is responsible—in his words, "overly responsible." He is the kind of person who likes to be given a general picture of what needs to be done. He then organizes himself, plans out the events, and completes the project on time. This style was not good enough for his boss, however. Clark wanted Thomas to do things *his* way. As time went on, Thomas discovered that other staff members felt stymied as well, but they were keeping their mouths shut. Most of the staff were there to meet their own needs, although initially many of them, like Thomas, had joined because they believed in the mission of the agency.

There was plenty of "dirt" on the floor, but everyone was stepping over it, afraid to confront the issues and the boss. Thomas would not compromise his values. "I'm a straight shooter!" Thomas exclaimed. "One of my talents is to *notice* what is going on and *do* something about it. I'm living a lie not to be my independent self—to say what's on my mind and help the cause."

Over a six-month period, Thomas and Clark had many opportunities to talk. Thomas felt that he was unfairly judged most of the time; the more he vied for his independence—to contribute in his way—the more punitive Clark became. Eventually, Thomas and Clark reached an impasse; Thomas's boss asked him to resign and offered him a one-month severance package.

Thomas sorted out his feelings. He was angry, and his ego was a little bruised because he hadn't submitted his resignation *first*. In our sessions, he yelled, "I couldn't stand the dirt on the floor!" and repeated this phrase several times. As things turned out, once he had vented his anger, Thomas recognized that "seeing the dirt on the floor" was one of his *assets*—an asset that he had honed over the years. I said to him, "Let's do some reframing. 'Seeing the dirt on the floor' means to me that you have an ability to see what the issues are and to give people feedback so that they can grow." Thomas's eyes lit up, and I asked, "Is this true?" "Yes," Thomas responded. "It's been the case throughout my life." I told Thomas that there are people who are paid to use this skill—counselors, psychologists, and other types of consultants, people paid for their insight and boldness. During the next couple of sessions, Thomas told me about how he had used this skill in a variety of instances. At his last job, for example, he had given feedback to managers about their coaching style with staff members. Now Thomas works *with* a management consulting firm. He is independent—using his best skills—and interdependent—working with a team where there is a mutual sense of value and purpose.

▧

Each one of us is responsible for generating our own creativity and ingenuity, but we are also responsible for helping others.

—B. J. Curry Spitler, founder and president, Age Concerns, Inc.

Honor Your Style

Let's go back to Thomas for a moment. Thomas was asked to resign; in other terms, he was fired. Initially, this was a mixed blessing. Thomas was ready for a change. During his three-month period of unemployment, he transformed himself by adapting and surviving. His efforts led to creating and succeeding. The roots of his success were deeply embedded in his style, or the patterns that best represented what he believed and the ways he performed his work. Thomas is an expressive person who needs to share his opinion and use his creativity to influence others. The best word I can think of to describe what Thomas felt and what other people like him feel when they are aware of and act on their style is *liberated*. They experience surges of energy and a sense of freedom to overcome everyday obstacles in pursuit of meaningful goals. This does not mean that all of a sudden, they are on easy street. On the contrary, your style and the expression of it are a responsibility. It is work, *and* it is a joy. It represents newfound power. The next question for Thomas—and maybe for you—is, "How are you going to harness your power? and for what purpose?"

Once you have found the words to express your style and you begin your search for meaningful work, it is almost impossible to turn back, although you may try. The truth is difficult to avoid. It is not uncommon to have fits and starts. To overcome obstacles and continue on your journey, I recommend that you build a "success and survival kit." Be sure to include in your kit people who will *listen* to you. You'll know people are listening when you are affirmed for your feelings and supported for doing what you need to do to press on in your job or career. A good listener might also make suggestions with your best interests in mind. People who are poor listeners will try to tell you who you are or what you *should* do next; that's *your* job. Are there people you trust who might be helpful to you?

Your Success and Survival Kit

A success and survival kit contains the tools (books, computer, brochures), people, and other support systems that are helpful to you when you're going through transition or when you're about to make some type of work or life change. Your kit might include your spouse, your best friend, a specific publication, a personal journal, a counselor, or a special place where you go to think. Be creative; anyone or anything that is helpful to you can be included in your kit.

On a separate sheet of paper or in your personal journal, write down who and/or what is in your success and survival kit. You can always change the contents of your kit and most likely you *will*, as you change.

1. Which trusted people might be helpful to you?

2. Which things could be helpful to you?

3. Where do you like go to think and renew yourself?

Loaning Yourself to the Organization

Your organization may be in the process of making radical changes, redesigning its products and services and redefining how it will do business. It could also be that your organization is now the right "working" size and structure—it has fewer layers, with workers who seem ready to produce. The organization, at least on the surface, is redeveloping and getting ready for business, so to speak. But are you?

You might be. But more likely, you've been working diligently— with your head down—throughout all the changes. Be careful not to bury yourself in the tasks at hand. Remember the bigger picture. Remember, your success and survival—and the organization's—are at stake. No one individual or organization can foresee or control outcomes. "I've got a good situation," commented Janice, an advertising account executive, "but we could lose a major deal and my job could be at stake." Reframe your work situation. Take an hour a week to schedule a meeting with yourself to do just that. If you're developing a "self-employed" attitude, you should be thinking, "I'm loaning myself and my competencies to an organization for a certain period of time"— advice offered by Julia O'Mara, coauthor of *Managing Workforce 2000: Gaining the Diversity Advantage*, during an interview with me.

Thinking this way can be liberating, even if you're not sure how it translates in the marketplace. Jobs may be scarce in your field, but what remains is the nature of today's work world. You'll have a job only for as long as you are providing a service—something that adds value within a niche that's yours—that someone will pay for. Knowing this, you can do your job *and* keep your eyes open for alternatives.

Personal redeveloping involves doing comprehensive research in order to make prudent business decisions. Therefore, if you're thinking about leaving your organization, you need to thoroughly examine your reasons and options. One consideration, often unrecognized, is that moving on doesn't have to mean leaving your organization. You have made an investment in your current organization, including the time you've spent getting to know the culture and colleagues, sharing your expertise, and contributing your knowledge. Realistically, if you did choose to leave, you would still be responsible for your job productivity and career mobility. There are no guarantees anywhere; you are still "self-employed," no matter what you decide.

Inspiration

Sheila was a training manager at a software company that was eliminating as many managers as possible in an effort to reduce costs and streamline operations. She was the chief financial provider for her family, and she wondered, "How can I save my job and be true to who I am?" First, she determined in what specific ways the company was changing. Her analysis revealed that the management training department would be slowly phased out. Sheila clarified and prioritized her core skills and decided that her consulting and project management skills would be valuable in the company's newly structured divisions. She rewrote her job description, presenting herself to her boss as a project manager who would consult with internal and external customers. She reframed her background and created another job in the same organization. Sheila planned to use this job as a bridge toward another position externally in the event that she decided to leave.

**Basically, there are three choices you can make.
You can choose perspiration—that's keeping your
head down and doing your work; desperation—
that's working as though the boom is going to drop
at any time; or inspiration—that's doing your work
and taking charge of your work life.**

*—R. Michael Sato, consultant and trainer,
RMS Organization Consulting and Training*

The Struggle Is Part of the Action

Most of you have been paid to do your jobs, not necessarily to think about and explain to others what you do for work. If you lost your job tomorrow, you would be thrust into the job marketplace or into your workplace's market. You would have to learn to explain clearly what you do and how your skills and abilities apply to a potential employer's or customer's needs. If you no longer wanted to do the same work or if the type of work you had been doing no longer existed, you would be faced with another type of personal redevelopment puzzle.

Whatever the case, you would want to create your best chance for doing what is *you*: work that reflects your skills, abilities, values, and passion. "I don't want to do the same old things; they bore me," claimed Ed, an accountant. "I'm fifty-one years old. It's time to shift my focus and feel excited about my work again. But this transition is difficult—the old ways no longer fit, and I'm unsure about where I'm headed." The struggle is part of personal redevelopment in action. It's a struggle to sit still and reevaluate yourself, especially when you've been rewarded for doing. Compounding the struggle is the nature of the current competitive and fluctuating job market. These claims bear some truth, but one of my clients asserted, "You've got to accept the struggle. It's part of getting to where you want to go. I've got to assess and evaluate who I am and what I want, or I'll always be scared about what might happen to me."

Exceeding Quota, But . . .

Steve, an account representative at a large consulting firm, has consistently exceeded quota and been viewed by his organization as successful. Steve himself, however, has been feeling underutilized—in his words, "unfulfilled." His job, as it is structured, uses only a small portion of his skill and potential. As he examined his deeper needs and tested future possibilities, Steve reported having several sleepless nights. He said, "Waking up to my needs and who I was kept me awake at night." The struggle to let go eventually became his gateway for moving on.

"We are all self-employed" is our new conscious reality, but living it doesn't come easily. "The journey is unpredictable," said Lisa, the editor-turned-scriptwriter. "Further," she continued, "there were times when I felt exhausted. Once I started on this path, I feared giving up. My greatest fear was that I would end up doing work again just to pay the bills. Understanding myself and pursuing work that I really wanted seemed so elusive at times."

Lisa found support and persevered. Now that she is working as a scriptwriter, she is feeling good about her accomplishment. She is challenged to write in a different way, producing scripts that can be adapted to video. In addition, she is aware that what she is doing today and her needs will change. Having made the move to scriptwriter has given her the confidence to see that she can assess her needs and manifest her goals and that she can make this process work again.

> **You cannot assign responsibility for your life to anyone.**
> **Life requires integrating self-information that no one else**
> **has . . . both intuitive and factual. You must keep on checking,**
> **"Is what I'm doing right for me?" This is not simple,**
> **because of internal and external variables.**
>
> —*Mark Campbell, manager of human resource planning*
> *and development, Northrop Corporation*

I'm Inviting Myself In

To sustain, renew, or aspire to competitive success, large and small organizations must reassess and change the ways they do and think about work. Many of these organizations have applied new methodologies—total quality management (TQM), reengineering, redeveloping, self-managing teamwork—to guide them through radical redesign or toward innovative processes. In fact, these methodologies have become much more than practical applications for solving problems. They have become ideologies—philosophies founded on specific tenets for transforming vision to reality, beliefs that transcend complexity and obstacles in order to achieve specific outcomes. The new systems have given us permission to rethink what we do and the language to communicate how we do what we do.

A new breed of pioneers are helping organizations to rediscover themselves and go beyond survival toward success. They have adopted a "self-employed" attitude; they are helping their organizational clients do the same. It is to Tom Peters's credit that we now "search for excellence"; Peter Senge steers us through a "learning" labyrinth, out of the classroom, into the boardroom, and throughout every function in the organization; Margaret Wheatley teaches us that chaos, as we see in nature, is necessary for growth; and David Nadler encourages us to rebuild our "organizational architecture," creating a framework for increasing productivity. These management experts have *invited themselves* into a global marketplace of change. Their timing is right.

Similarly, Len, a divisional general manager at a food manufacturing conglomerate, noticed, "I *was* invited in. But now, I'm inviting myself in. The former president used to direct the show, and basically, we would follow. High-priced followers! In contrast, the new president expects the general managers to initiate—share ideas and participate in decision making." From now on, Len will need to recognize problems, suggest where costs can be cut, and decide when to institute new programs or expand existing ones. With fewer workers, increased workloads, and greater pressure to innovate and perform, Len must learn a new management philosophy and strategy. His learning is not only about how to manage others but also about how to manage his own career at work. Len must reconsider how to take personal risks, especially at his level; to sharpen his awareness of what needs to be done; and to test the relevancy of his ideas.

The closer you are to who you are, the more responsibility and empowerment you have.

Conscious Loneliness Is Part of the Journey

Undeniably, we each—alone—must face ourselves and the changes we must make. We can surround ourselves with other people and things to do and hope that others will know us better than we know ourselves. Or we can cling to past beliefs and archaic organizational values and norms, only to one day find that our growth has been retarded, that we have been stymied by our fear of loneliness—as though loneliness were something to be avoided at all costs. In *Man's Search for Himself,* Rollo May comments on the characteristic threat of loneliness: "When one's customary way of orienting oneself is threatened, and one is without other selves around one, one is thrown back on inner resources and inner strength, and this is what modern people have neglected to develop. Hence loneliness is a real, not imaginary, threat to many of them."[2]

For a moment, think about a recent change in your work life and about the inner resources you used to make this change.

≣ *What is one activity that you have given up in the past twelve months?*

≣ *What are you doing now instead of this activity?*

≣ *What inner resources did you use to make a successful transition?*

≣ *What would you discover if—just temporarily—you were not distracted by television, friends, colleagues, organizational boundaries, self-deprecating thoughts?*

≣ *What would you uncover if you took your precious time—ten minutes, two hours, or a weekend—to begin thinking about your life and what you really want?*

≣ *What would happen if you committed to a self-inspired journey that included unavoidable emptiness—fibers woven into the rich texture of the fabric of self-discovery?*

With patience, persistence, tolerance, and learning, you would *live* your life—the process—and achieve goals that were meaningful to you. You would serve yourself and others. You would be happier.

We tend to be alive in the future, not now.
—*Thich Nhat Hanh*, Being Peace

When I think about my own times of loneliness, not aloneness, I am in touch with an empty feeling, as though I am missing something—as though there is little present when I allow myself to be still, undistracted. After I adjust to the stillness, I can feel my heartbeat and experience air passing in and out of my body, and sometimes I am alarmed at how shallow my breathing is. I walk into the emptiness, when I give myself permission to be lonely, and I don't judge this experience through the lens of our "Instamatic" culture. I see myself coming toward myself, as if I am having an out-of-body experience.

Objectively, I come to a point of identifying areas in which I need to grow and accept my need to learn—take risks. I accept my need as growth—life—not as an impediment but as a challenge, a chance to foster my independence. I can see, for example, that I need to follow my own dreams. It is when I try to follow others or cling to others in some way that I feel most anxious and derailed from myself. If I give myself a chance in the empty, lonely times, eventually I find myself in fuller times. As Thomas observed, "I've got to be who I am and do what I need to do." Loneliness happens to be part of the journey—for everybody.

Unconscious Loneliness

As Rollo May has said, "The clearest picture of the empty life is the suburban man who gets up at the same hour every weekday morning, takes the same train to work in the city, performs the same tasks in the office, lunches in the same place, leaves the same tip for the waitress each day, comes home on the same train each night . . . and moves through a routine, a mechanical existence year after year until he finally retires at sixty-five and very soon thereafter dies of heart failure, possibly brought on by repressed hostility. I have always had a secret suspicion, however, that he dies of boredom."[3]

We have no choice but consciousness. As the chains of boredom were strapped on to many workers, our society was slowly being broken; today that's the way our society *is*.

Getting Paid: No Guarantees

A "self-employed" attitude includes emotional, psychological, philosophical, and social factors. And let's not forget the economic factor—getting paid! According to the November 1, 1993, issue of *Fortune*, "A survey of more than 2,000 U.S. companies by Hewitt Associates, a compensation consulting firm, documents a remarkable trend. Since 1988 the number of U.S. concerns offering variable pay, chiefly bonuses, to all salaried employees has jumped from 47% to 68%. Moreover, these companies now pay out far more in incentive compensation than in salary increases."[4] Incentive compensation is based on results—pay-for-performance. But not all organizations or executives see or respect this trend. At a financial services company, the president gathered his top executives for a meeting. The agenda was to discuss "compensation." At the time, the executives were paid a "guaranteed" bonus—an amount, up to a particular percentage, *promised* to each executive beyond his or her salary. The president proposed that the executives consider an incentive compensation package instead. Rather than a guaranteed bonus, the executives were presented with an appreciably larger incentive: the opportunity to commit more deeply to joining in the process of running the company, as if they owned a share of the business. At year's end, the executives' contributions would be judged against predetermined goals. If they met their goals, they would be paid an amount for their contribution and an additional amount based on the performance of the company as a whole. Self-employed workers are paid this way, and, as many of you know, sometimes they don't get paid at all, or not as much as in previous years. Pay-for-performance: This is the real world.

In the financial services company discussed above, it is interesting to note that when the ballots were counted, the executives chose safety over adventure—that is, to retain the compensation system of guaranteed bonuses. Their choice may work for them in the short term because the company is doing well, but paradoxically, safety—guaranteed bonuses—is no longer a safety at all. The president had offered his executives a challenge: to look at themselves, to become more accountable for their actions, and to learn a new way to be successful and in greater harmony with the world. Next time, I believe, these workers won't have a choice. Why should anyone get paid for anything else but performance—doing his or her job—serving others?

The Outlook

The world and our lives will always be in constant flux. If you're thinking, "Stop the world! I want to get off," I can see why. Managerial jobs will continue to disappear. Career ladders will continue to crumble. "Challenge" will replace "promotions." Many more workers will see themselves and be seen as temporary consultants and project managers working to resolve problems and invent solutions. Companies will continue to break up into smaller, specialized entities. Minibusinesses, serving larger businesses and one another, will dot the frontier.

Personal, professional, and global learning will be continuous for all of us. Our commitment to learning—discovering and taking risks—will prepare us for inevitable and invaluable change. Learning as a graded, classroom activity will become only an initial indoctrination for most people. Learning will have no walls. Security will be redefined; you will need to learn how to integrate your two-part job description—your professional job and the job of "career self-manager"—on an ongoing basis. As the next chapter points out, many workers will create work that is meaningful to them and others. The bottom line is that every worker will rethink or be forced to rethink and reshape his or her job or career.

When you are "self-employed," you are creating ownership—
pushing decision making down to where the opportunity is.
It's not easy, because it's not easy for leaders to give up control
and people on the front lines are not used to taking control.
Leaders and managers must risk and relinquish control.
We must reward risk taking, and people must accept ownership.

—*Bob Gill, service manager, Polaroid Corporation*

CREATING
MEANINGFUL WORK

Work, believing that the world offers what you need
and that you can make a contribution

EMPLOYED ATTITUDE

Dependent Mindset

What I do doesn't really matter. I'm just doing a job. I bring my body
to work and leave my spirit behind.

SELF-EMPLOYED ATTITUDE

Independent and Interdependent Mindset

I will create meaningful work. I am resourceful and able to give value
to my work—to market my skills, negotiate for my needs, and make a
contribution regardless of my job or level.

IN THE PAST CENTURY, OUR ECONOMY HAS CHANGED its
focus, from farming and manufacturing to service and technology.
Despite our enormous advances and burgeoning knowledge, we
face increasingly dire societal problems and challenges, including vio-
lence, drugs, hunger, joblessness, and apathy. Creating meaningful
work—using our imaginations and taking risks along the path of discovery, growth, and contribution—has been essential to our cultural
legacy and development. Now more than ever, we need to stretch our
imaginations and open our minds to new questions and unexpected
answers. Those who are asleep must awaken and do their part: first, to
know themselves, and second, to add value to the world in some
way—in *their* way—despite the obstacles.

This chapter illustrates, through a series of vignettes, what some
people have accomplished by embracing a "self-employed" attitude:
creating work that is meaningful to them and to others. These stories
are of a variety of workers, representing a broad range of professions.
Each has opted for the job of "career self-manager," a concept discussed throughout this book. All have taken control of their careers; all
add value to their organizations, customers, and clients; all seek and
find work that is meaningful to them. In this chapter, these individuals
share their insights and practices. The career and life choices they have
made required courage; collectively, their stories demonstrate that you

too can develop a "self-employed" attitude—one of integrity, responsibility, and both independence and interdependence.

Whether you are a company worker, a business owner, a part-time worker, an unchallenged worker, a laid-off worker, an early-retired or never-want-to-retire worker, or a recent college graduate, you *can* develop a "self-employed" attitude. As you take responsibility for your job productivity and career mobility and for serving others, you will increase your self-respect, develop your inner strength, gain your independence, experience interdependence (not dependence), feel happier, enjoy financial success, and make a contribution.

On the next two pages are detailed the "characteristics of meaningful work" and the "skills for creating meaningful work." These characteristics and skills represent a synthesis of collective wisdom shared by the people whom I interviewed for this chapter. This information provides the framework and guidelines for you to examine your current work situation and skills. After you've reviewed these lists, you will have valuable information that you can use to create more meaningful work.

Company Workers

Paul H. P. Christen

LAN Support Specialist

Addison-Wesley Publishing Company

The way Paul got his most recent promotion illustrates his "self-employed" attitude. Basically, he assumed a role as a LAN (Local Area Network) support specialist, a position he had wanted unofficially before it was officially offered to him. Paul noticed that LAN had a leading role in the ways Addison-Wesley communicated internally and externally with customers and service providers. In the publishing

Characteristics of Meaningful Work

Which of the characteristics are present in your work now? Strive toward achieving the ones that are not.

- I'm collaborating with others. As a result, I'm understanding what others need, improving my skills, and developing new ones.

- My life feels reasonably balanced among my work, family, social, and spiritual needs.

- My values are respected.

- I can show my enthusiasm and express, not suppress, my authentic self.

- I feel that my work is an integrated part of me and my life, not an appendage to it.

- Despite obstacles, I am productive and committed to making a contribution.

- Money is not the purpose of my work; rather, it is fuel for fulfilling my purpose.

Skills for Creating Meaningful Work

Take note of your proficiencies, and work on the skills that you feel need improvement.

I have the ability to . . .

- take risks based on what I know and believe.
- assess myself.
- learn from feedback.
- prioritize my needs.
- listen to others.
- understand the needs of others.
- recognize opportunity.
- research an opportunity to determine if it is sufficiently meaningful for me to pursue it.
- differentiate myself—develop a niche, a valued service.
- defer gratification and maintain the discipline necessary to work incrementally toward my goal.
- change my plan—but not my vision—in order to reach my goals.
- ask for guidance and support.
- talk with myself in an encouraging manner in order to overcome obstacles.
- articulate what I have to offer and share my plan.
- take responsibility for my actions.
- respond to priorities.
- talk with other influential people about my needs.
- sell my ideas to others.
- reflect on my mistakes and successes and learn from them.
- reward myself for taking risks and staying the course.

business, these people include authors, editors, fulfillment and shipping service people, and production and design support personnel.

"Essentially," Paul explained, "I volunteered my expertise to make the LAN system more accessible to users by, for example, writing a training manual and resource guide and giving seminars on its use. As I took on these responsibilities, I checked in with my boss to let him know what I was doing. I also asked him, 'Where do you see this project going in the future?' His answers helped me to sort through my own questions: 'Will *I* be able to carry this project into the future?' and 'Do I *want* to do this project as my future?' " Paul's timing was right, the answers to his questions were positive, and by *doing* the job, he *got* the job.

Patricia Stimpson
Director of Working Together Development
Lotus Development

For the past twenty-four years, Patricia has contributed to the field of software development as an engineer, manager, and director of engineers. She began her career at Harvard Business School, where she built the simulation game that is used by second-year MBA students. She later worked at start-up and *Fortune* 500 companies, such as Wang Laboratories and Nixdorf Computer.

In the early 1980s, Patricia realized that she was longing to find more significance in her life. "Life," in her words, "had to have a deeper purpose than my job and raising children. I was feeling a hollowness; part of myself was not feeling fully developed. I was using my brain; I was a new mother; but part of me was not being enriched." She began to explore her spiritual values—love, peace, oneness: collaboration rather than competition. While at her full-time job at Wang in 1987, she started a spiritual business called Abundance, which taught adults about aspects of spiritual living. During the day, she managed engineers; in the evening, she ran Abundance. "But," she said, "seven years later, I felt fragmented. I wasn't fully bringing my passion to either place. I got as far as I could in each world. I couldn't go forward until I pulled these parts of myself into one."

Patricia chose one of her worlds: She decided that she would bring her spirit—her passion—to the business world. "I wanted to take on a role of solving an unsolvable problem," she said; "I did not want a traditional role that already existed." One such problem, for example, was getting product teams to work together. This meant that engineers would need to learn how to share the codes used for building a product. "I spent five months," Patricia reflected, "trying to convince senior management that this or another such problem could be solved. They were having a hard time making up their minds. In the meantime, I was offered a job at a start-up and accepted. On the day I was leaving, a senior manager at Lotus came forward with a problem."

The manager wanted Patricia to redevelop all of Lotus's software products so they functioned to help people collaborate, share, and work together in groups. In mid-May 1993, Patricia began building a team and implementing the program. She chose the title "Director of Working Together Development" because it reflected her new challenge, to make software that helps customers work together. "Working together" is also a universal Lotus Development marketing phrase. To implement the working-together strategy, first engineers had to learn to work together, or, as Patricia remarked, "to learn 'oneness.' Engineers were accustomed to working as cowboys [lone practitioners]. Instead, we needed to look for ways to benefit one another. We also learned that we could inspire and be resources to one another." This was the working-together strategy—the spirit—that Patricia's team would build into the software.

If managers and team members said to Patricia, "We can't do this," she would respond, "I believe, with your help, we can reach our goal." Part of her spiritual teaching involved encouraging others to share their ideas. People felt more included and rose to the challenge. Patricia's choices and beliefs have led her to integrate spirit and business. Some of the changes she has seen as a result are reflected in the following comparative list:

Before	*Now*
Engineers would say, "I want to do it this way." They would not look at their impact on others.	Engineers ask, "How is my behavior going to affect others?" They believe that *they* need to share in order to build a product that facilitates sharing among others.
In the company, younger people were valued because they could work eighty hours a week.	There is more balance. Older people are valued for their patience, perseverance, and negotiating skills, and younger people are valued for their drive and energy.
Left-brain—logical—skills were rewarded.	Right-brain—creative, people-oriented—skills are seen as valuable too.
Aggressive people got attention.	Quieter people are seen as bringing another aspect to the job. Some customers, for example, respond better to a less aggressive approach.

From July to December 1993, Lotus's stock value increased approximately thirty points. As of January 1994, it was hovering in the high fifties. During the two years prior to implementation of the working-together strategy, the press was predicting that Lotus wouldn't make it. Since June 1993, the press has been very favorable. Patricia has proved that a "self-employed" attitude can be good for everyone—colleagues, senior management, customers, stockholders, *and* herself.

John Rogener

Program Director, Financial Institutions Transaction

   Services Training Department

Citicorp/Citibank

Citicorp/Citibank provides transaction services for other financial institutions, such as banks, insurance companies, and brokerage firms. John received a mandate to train 1,700 people in "object-oriented technology." The more he looked at the technology, the more he sensed that training 1,700 people would not net the desired results. John commented, "The method was a silver bullet; it lacked breadth."

John demonstrated his "self-employed" attitude when he challenged the system and expressed his creativity. His approach was not to take things at face value but to see things creatively—to look at problems and issues from different perspectives. "I like to take a regular sheet of paper and turn it sideways," John said. "I like to crumple it up and try new ways of seeing that paper. I do a lot with looking at things differently. I also look at the ripple effects of a particular plan. I ask, 'If we go with this plan, what will the impact be on the organization and others?' Change can be a pain in the neck because it often creates stress and work."

When he analyzed the potential effectiveness of training 1,700 people, John influenced others, over time, to change the mission. Instead, he and his team now provide varied and smaller-scale training and development support services to his clients, and the results are excellent. "Bottom line?" John said, "You have to believe in yourself. You must be responsible for your own decisions rather than letting the institution dictate to you. I ask, 'In the event that the institution is not there anymore, what will I do?' What I always come back to is 'I'm going to make the most of *this* experience.' "

Robert L. Fulford
Purchasing Manager
Varian Ion Implant Systems

If you are manifesting a "self-employed" attitude, you, as was the case for Robert, are likely to earn your boss's confidence. Robert stated, "It's as though I don't have a boss; I'm my own boss. I take full responsibility, consistently, for managing the purchasing process."

Robert also went beyond his job responsibilities. One year, for example, he volunteered to take an active role in the development of the New England Suppliers Institute (NESI), a collection of large private and public businesses and state and federal agencies dedicated to assisting smaller businesses to produce and deliver higher-quality goods more effectively and efficiently. Robert, along with other steering committee members, took the initiative to provide training as a means of upgrading workers' skills. As a result of their efforts, the committee hoped to develop jobs and to sustain and increase long-term growth within the member companies and their supply base.

The freedom Robert earned at Varian Ion Implant Systems and his involvement with NESI are two examples of his ability to partner. He is challenged by staying flexible. "Every day," Robert remarked, "I come in and develop what it is I do. With more to do and fewer people to do it with, I've learned to respond to customer priorities."

Business Owners

E. Janice Leeming

President

About Women, Inc.

Janice began her career as a venture capitalist, and her passion led her to buying About Women, Inc., an organization that provides companies with the information they need to become more successful in their marketing efforts to women. In her work life, Janice has learned that "there is real danger in standing still. There are two fears that I have: the fear of going forward and the fear of standing still. I choose going forward."

Janice's successful career can be traced back to her family roots. Her father, like my grandfather, had no high school education. He managed 200 people in a manufacturing plant; he burned the grass. Janice said, "He taught me to be fair—to treat people well. People responded to him because he worked hard, expected others to work hard, and was himself fair." Janice continued, "My mother was an inspiration. She would say, 'Focus on the positives. Do a job that emphasizes the positive aspects of life.' My mother wasn't afraid of anything." The combination of her father's work ethic and her mother's attitude has inspired Janice to live a "self-employed" attitude.

During a fifteen-year period, Janice worked at two venture capital firms and rose to the level of vice-president. The venture capital business "is very deal-oriented," she commented. "It is made up of lone deal makers." She decided she needed more in her life than searching for the next Apple Computer. With the mission in mind to invest in companies owned and operated by women, Janice then started Leeming Investments. She said, "I ran my company for two years, then I discovered About Women, Inc. I liked the business, saw there was potential, 'put my money were my mouth is,' and bought it." Starting her own venture capital business was a risky but significant step to finding work that was more collaborative.

Janice wanted to build consensus with groups—collaborate and brainstorm—and she wanted to be more helpful to people and organizations. About Women, Inc., became an opportunity to do something with and for women and to earn money. "Now," Janice said, "I help to make advertising genuinely more representative of the evolving woman. Through a great deal of research, we discover who women are and what they want and need. Our newsletter, *Marketing to Women*, is a byproduct of the research we do."

Universal Pictures, Gillette, the *Wall Street Journal*, Saint Helena Hospital—these are but a few subscribers to *Marketing to Women*. "Our clients," remarked Janice, "learn 'who the woman is out there.' We answer such questions as 'Are women optimistic about the economy?' 'How are women feeling about the economy? controlled health care costs? the budget and unemployment?' 'How important are nutrition and health care?' " Answers to these questions give her clients ideas for both developing new products and creating new ways to influence purchasing decisions by women.

Janice confessed that running her own business is difficult; she felt, however, that working at something one doesn't believe in is even more difficult. She said, "If you believe in what you are doing, you'll find the resources to keep on going." Janice's undergraduate degree in psychology and her MBA in finance, plus her experience in the venture capital business, are only part of her success equation. The other part is more elusive for most workers. She stated, "My advice to my children and others is 'Do what you enjoy and find easy. Work does not have to be hard. We all have talent that we push away. Don't stop because you think it looks too easy.' "

James J. Cantillon
Financial and Business Consultant
Cantillon & Associates

The partners in the architectural firm where Jim worked went through a "divorce." Jim said, "This altered the complexion of the business; my job as controller was eliminated."

It took Jim approximately six months from the time he was laid off to reach the point of starting Cantillon & Associates, a company that consults to architectural and engineering firms on their financial activities—accounting systems and their financial policies, analyses, and planning. To get there, his path was far from linear. Jim commented, "Like so many others who work on a daily basis, I got caught up in the doing. When I lost my job, although it was not my first inclination, I stepped back from looking for a job or starting a job search. First, I needed to assess my values and skills and decide where to apply them." Jim told himself that it was "OK to feel frightened." His self-reassurance contributed to assessing his strengths and to undertaking a networking effort.

At first, Jim's exploration led him to investigate a variety of industries and larger corporations. But other industries were hard to break into, and larger corporations, for Jim, didn't feel right. "It was," Jim said, "by happenstance in the first place that I landed in the business of supporting architects and engineers. When I explored other industries, I learned that I was service-oriented, as opposed to being someone who worked *for* a manufacturer. I also learned that my happenstance made sense: I had particular value in the architectural and engineering field; there were many smaller firms that could use my financial expertise and understanding of their particular field; further, there was no one like me who offered 'controllership services' to this industry."

Jim was in a good position to build on what he had done in the past. With one major exception, he did not want to work in a single firm. As Jim networked and compared against his own values what other people said and did, he learned that "variety" was a fundamental value to him. He didn't like repetition and routine, but he did like solving problems. Jim proclaimed, "I made the shift from 'looking for a job' to 'marketing my services.' I didn't have to be confined to full-time employment." Jim manifested a "self-employed" attitude when he expanded his thinking and beliefs. Rather than working in one firm as a controller, today he has established a niche. He said, "On a part-time basis, I help architects and engineers to balance the difference between achieving design excellence and running a profitable business venture."

Assuming that you are doing what you want to be doing and that your work is relevant in the changed marketplace, if you lose your job, the shortest route to reemployment for you, as it was for Jim, is to reassess what your skills and values are and where to apply them next. "A main problem for many," Jim said, "is their comfort with the status quo. They hope for the best, but this keeps them in place and therefore they stagnate. They go on thinking, 'I do what the boss tells me to do.'" Workers today cannot allow others to take control of their careers.

When I asked Jim which of his lessons he wanted to pass on to others, he said, "Employers don't look after employees; they look after their bottom line. They 'reengineer' to make a profit. Everyone needs to know that 'no change is no good.' "

Part-Time Workers

Deborah F. Mulloy

Nurse Manager

University Hospital

Deborah began, "What I do is to job-share with a partner. Job sharing is a full-time commitment to get our work done. Job sharing involves being totally committed to serving the organization, colleagues, and staff, and at the same time attending to your own needs."

Deborah partners with Joanne, her colleague, to manage a nursing staff. They agreed that Deborah would work approximately sixteen hours a week; Joanne, twenty-four hours a week. This configuration allowed Deborah time to attend to her family, teach nursing, and consult for private industry. For Joanne, the arrangement gave her an opportunity to work and simultaneously pursue a master's degree.

Perseverance and patience were among Deborah's "self-employed" attributes that contributed to achieving her goal. She'd spent six years at University Hospital before making the change from full-time manager to job sharer, a change that unfolded over a year-long period. Most important, she knew that she liked her job, wanted to stay at University Hospital, and had worked hard to grow into this management role. But she also knew that with two children and other personal considerations, she needed to restructure her work. Her first step was to do a literature search on job sharing. "My goal," Deborah recalled, "was to understand the benefits of job sharing for myself and for the hospital. This involved doing a library information search and reading cases about how others successfully went about the process."

Deborah learned that the hospital could greatly benefit by joining her in the effort to redesign her management role. The hospital would gain a higher level of productivity from two people who were committed to this role than from one forty-hour person. In addition, with their team approach to problem solving, Deborah and Joanne would contribute highly applicable methods and expand the number of creative solutions. Moreover, they would not be distracted from their jobs by other life concerns. And Deborah and Joanne both brought their specific and cumulative areas of expertise as well as their excitement and dedication to their work and to the hospital.

Deborah feels that healthy job sharing is cardinal to a "self-employed" attitude. She is able to meet her needs and contribute to the lives of others. Deborah attributes her job-sharing success to many factors, although one vital component stands out: *communication.* "Communication," she said, "is vital with staff, between Joanne and me, and with hospital administration. Joanne and I are both determined to make this work, so we tape-record messages to each other every day. We also reviewed our job description so that our responsibilities were clearly defined and all objectives could be met. For example, Joanne is responsible for long-term scheduling, and I focus on daily crisis intervention, such as when staff call in sick. This not only helps us communicate effectively but also sends a clear message to staff about which one of us they should come to to discuss their needs."

Deborah's case offers a superb example of joining, not working for, your organization and customers. She supports Joanne in her work and feels that she mentors Joanne in her educational pursuits. In turn, Joanne encourages Deborah at work and on the home front. University Hospital, staff, and customers are the recipients of their successful joint effort. Deborah reminded all those interested in adopting a "self-employed" attitude, "It's not always easy, but go after what you want."

Sy Friedlander
Psychologist, Manager, Teacher, and Consultant

Sy Friedlander has woven a career tapestry of several part-time jobs that interrelate, maximize his skills and abilities, and provide expression for his passion. As of this writing, Sy's job titles have included director of quality assurance for a human service agency, interim executive director of a social service agency, consultant to a school system, and teacher of graduate students in the area of psychological assessment.

Sy commented, "I have expressed a 'self-employed' attitude by becoming more comfortable with my generic skills. They include healing, negotiating, mending, making others feel comfortable, and helping others to see the win-win value in collaboration. I have mobility in my career because I know what I do best and am learning how to apply it to marketplace needs. Rather than trying to fit myself into a job opening, I have learned to first assess what I have and *want* to contribute. Then I evaluate how my skills and desires add value in the marketplace."

In one situation, for example, Sy facilitated a collaborative relationship between two health care agencies. As a result, the agencies established a greater geographic range and expanded their customer bases. In addition, they contributed their specific areas of expertise to each other, enhancing the skills of professional staff and the delivery of service to patients.

Working as a clinical psychologist, mainly doing psychological assessments, was too narrow for Sy. Adopting a "self-employed" attitude helped Sy reframe his background, thereby allowing him to enjoy a multifaceted career that utilizes his core skills and values.

Marcia Felth

Senior Consultant/Business Program Manager

Digital Equipment Corporation

Prior to taking what she called a "U-turn" in her work life, Marcia developed a twelve-year career in high-tech telecommunications management and planning. She worked at New England Telephone, Dennison Manufacturing Company, and Honeywell. Currently she works at Digital Equipment Corporation.

While at Honeywell, she managed thirty-four people and a budget of $20 million. She was recognized as one of 5 percent of the workforce to be named "high-potential talent"; she was someone to be watched. In 1986 she became pregnant, an event that started, in her words, "the great U-turn in my career." With a family, she felt the need to redefine her potential in terms other than those of work achievement. Marcia remarked, "It was tough for me to slow my career down. I felt pressure to live up to the expectations of my bosses, colleagues, and associates."

Marcia acted on her "self-employed" attitude by taking more control of two directions in order to attain a better balance between her work and her home life. She changed jobs and companies, leaving the pressure of the manager position at Honeywell to go to Digital as a high-level technical architect. In this role, she shed her direct responsibility for others to become a staff member. She looked three to five years toward the future at global and customer changes and needs and their relevancy to the telecommunications industry to predict and define what innovations lay ahead. She applied this research to solving business problems and developing strategies for Digital's technologies.

After the birth, in 1989, of Marcia's second child, Marcia asked her boss to reduce her hours to thirty per week, and her boss agreed. Marcia commented, "I lost sleep over going from forty to thirty hours per week." For years, working forty-plus hours per week had contributed to her definition of self as a fully committed, competent, determined worker. Making a decision to reduce her hours meant an adjustment period in order to redefine what success meant to her. In the same way that she was praised at Honeywell, Marcia was recognized at Digital for her contributions. Early in 1992, however, Digital began laying off workers—and Marcia *asked* to be laid off! She needed more time with her family and more personal time. Marcia stated, "My boss responded, 'You're a top performer; I can't lay you off. What else can I do for you?' " Today Marcia is working twenty hours per week. Part of her job involves workforce planning for the information technology group. She helps the group to define the skills, behaviors, and knowledge that will be necessary for performance management, future training, succession planning, and hiring. For Marcia, this work is highly meaningful, reflecting back to her aptitudes and graduate studies in career development.

I've elaborated on some of Marcia's work and life history to demonstrate that living a "self-employed" attitude—successfully creating, anticipating, and managing the U-turns in your life—takes time, patience, and cumulative learning. Marcia redefined success in terms of her own values during a seven-year period. And, as Marcia reminded me, "My journey is not going to stop. I'm always trying the next thing, and it all fits together."

I encourage clients to develop a personal "golden template" as a means for expressing their "self-employed" attitude. As mentioned in chapter 2, this template, or tool, is written in the form of a statement or constellation of statements. It represents a clear expression of any or all of the following: personal values, philosophy, skills, and aptitudes. You can refer to your golden template as you evaluate, create, and respond to opportunities.

Marcia's Golden Template

I will . . .

≣ learn what is important to me.

≣ define success in terms of my own values:

Integrity—I want to express my best self. This is who I am.

Family—I want to be accessible to my family without throwing my self away.

Challenge—I want to achieve and keep on learning.

Unchallenged Workers

Stanley W. Bartlett

*Environmental Design/*Feng Shui *Master and Consultant*

Bartlett Group

Stanley applied his "self-employed" attitude by taking responsibility for his spiritual awakening. "In the past," Stanley commented, "I was in *Who's Who*, chairman of this and president of that; I had a lavish lifestyle—the big house, yacht, and country-club membership." To outsiders, Stanley was successful beyond most people's dreams. But Stanley felt, "So what? Intuitively, I knew there must be something else."

Now, using *feng shui*, Stanley helps people achieve harmonious design in their homes and businesses, resulting in greater health, wealth, and good fortune. Translated as "wind and water," *feng shui* (pronounced *fung shway*) is an ancient art and science that seeks to balance the vital energy in humans (*chi*) with the forces of nature in their surroundings. *Feng shui* has been used in Asia for more than 4,000 years to design buildings and interiors. The renowned architect I. M. Pei, for example, used *feng shui* to design the mammoth Bank of China.

Feng shui, according to Stanley, has also been "used in homes to solve problems, from persistent headaches to familial fighting to dwindling bank accounts. Techniques or 'cures' used in the process range from making sure a bed is placed to provide the occupant with the widest possible view of the entrance of the bedroom to ensuring the kitchen stove (the wealth area of the home) is in a spacious, brightly lit, and well-ventilated area."[1]

Stanley explained, "The 'self-employed' concept relates to self-empowerment. All of my work deals with helping people connect with their divine, inner strength. I teach people how to balance outside [their environment] with inside [who they are and/or who they are becoming]." Stanley lives what he teaches. He expresses himself every day and everywhere.

Jan Nickerson
Managing Director
The Prosperity Collaborative

Jan consults with businesses, associations, and individuals on socially responsible management and marketing strategies. She helps them manage the dual bottom line of principles and profits with the understanding that money and profits are not the goal but the fuel for fulfilling these clients' purpose.

For twenty-one years prior to founding the Prosperity Collaborative, Jan worked in corporations in a variety of financial positions, ranging from auditor and CPA at Arthur Anderson Consulting to manager of accounting and internal audit at Incoterm to chief financial officer at Chase Access Services to vice-president of finance at Loyalty Management Group. Jan stated, "My philosophy has always been 'I am self-employed.' Working in these corporations, I learned I could not be self-employed in the ways that I wanted to be. My colleagues and bosses saw finance as a narrow, technical field designed to account for profit and loss. The technical aspect didn't challenge me. My challenge was in taking a global view. I saw finance as a major part of an organization's communications system that extended into the community; it lets us know how we are doing."

Jan's global view benefited the stakeholders of the business—who they were and what they needed. Stakeholders of a business enterprise are customers, workers, community, environment, government, suppliers, and financial investors. A global view, in Jan's opinion, involves the stakeholders in the running and development of the business. She asked them, "What do you need of us?" Then she drafted goals and objectives that incorporated their needs. Although her methods were disconcerting to others in the corporation, she was expressing her "self-employed" attitude and her global view.

Two situations acted as the catalysts in Jan's life for pursuing more meaningful work. In the first instance, the company she worked with had promised the workers that they would receive bonuses of a specific dollar amount. After the workers produced outstanding results, the board changed the rules, reneging on the agreement. The board said, "We call the shots." Jan could no longer work at a company that did not collaborate and that lacked integrity. "My spirit left after this incident," Jan commented. "My body stayed one more year so I could sort out the rest of my life. I put in minimal effort and produced totally satisfactory results. The company missed out on having me. I gave them my tools, not my spirit."

In the second situation, Jan was, for a while, able to do her work from a global perspective. She was not just a numbers person; in addition, she developed programs that, for example, reduced turnover from 33 to 10 percent. But the CEO had a problem with her enthusiasm. He said, "Do your job. Leave your enthusiasm at home." Jan, however, could not do so. She said, "My enthusiasm is my essence, my core. You get me, you get my enthusiasm."

The Prosperity Collaborative has become another expression of her "self-employed" attitude. One of her clients, the CEO of a manufacturing company, wants workers in the company to have more vitality. Jan thus coaches the management team to relinquish some of their control to the other workers. Consequently, workers are now participating in the development of the business. Work-team members on the factory floor talk about and figure out how to get a quality product out the door. The entire climate is far different from workers saying, "I've done my part; I'm waiting for the manager to make a decision."

Jan gives to others what is most meaningful to her: workplaces where people love to work, where spirit and passion are present.

Laid-off Workers

Jacek A. Nowicki
Formerly a Solutions Engineer at Digital Equipment Corporation
Currently Provides Services to Companies Interested
in Foreign Trade Ventures

Jacek said, "The fall of the titans [large companies] forced me out of corporate America. I learned that I had to go to the end of a very long line to get employment . . . and I wasn't willing to go to the end."

Jacek asserted a simple-sounding but ultimately profound thought that poignantly reflects a "self-employed" attitude. While attending a seminar on the global economy, he suddenly realized, "*I* am unique, and so is everyone else." "In my case," he mused, "I am fluent in four languages—English, Polish, Dutch, and French—and I'm multicultural; I've lived in different countries." For Jacek, understanding and embracing his uniqueness were crucial—as they are for you. He knew he had to—and learned he wanted to—differentiate himself in the highly competitive marketplace.

Jacek's business cards said, "Foreign Trade Services." "My focus," he explained, "is to boost people over barriers to foreign trade." Jacek chose not to call himself a "consultant," a noun, because it was limiting. He did not want to include himself with the thousands of laid-off corporate workers who were using the label "consultant" to hide the fact that they were unemployed or in transition. The label "consultant" can, however, serve as a bridge between unemployment and employment for some laid-off workers.

One of the first assignments Jacek found was as the interpreter between a U.S. firm and a Polish company. "I brought them to closure," he said, "by asking each party if they would accept a letter of intent to do business with each other. They developed the letters simultaneously, in two languages. Writing the letters in their respective languages integrated their thinking, exposed the ways each party thought, and created a bond between them."

At age fifty-five, Jacek chose "inspiration" to broaden his thinking, to reach deeply into his roots, to become self-examining, to activate and generate a live network, and to move to the *front* of the line.

Lisbeth Wiley Chapman
Principal/Consultant
Ink&Air

The marketing department changed, the new team leader wanted to bring in his own people and Lisbeth's job was at risk. Laid off from a major financial institution as vice-president of public relations, Lisbeth stated, "My journey was very scary. I am a single parent with a huge financial obligation. I wasn't going to let my sons down or lose my

house. And I was no longer willing to depend on the corporation."
Lisbeth had been divorced five years earlier. She had no savings; she
had no marital assets to fall back on. She lamented, "It was do or die."

Lisbeth had anticipated the coming layoff, and so while she was
still employed, she began a five-month grieving process and joined a
support group. During this period, she got in touch with her emotions
and felt better. Often the two processes go hand in hand. "I got angry,"
admitted Lisbeth, "because I wasn't being rewarded for my loyalty,
intensity, and hard work." She realized that she was a natural salesperson *and* that she could make money at it. When her work-life transition was over, she had named her new business. Today she is still part
of a group, an advisory board that supports its members through personal and professional transition.

Now, as sole proprietor of a niche public relations firm, she targets
the financial industry and is rewarded for her "loyalty, intensity, and
hard work." "My intensity," she proclaimed, "was hard to manage in a
corporate setting. As a small-business practitioner, I can use my intensity. It's one of my greatest assets." Lisbeth, for example, interviews all
of her clients for two to three hours before she begins working with
them. Then she writes a positioning audit so that her clients are clear
about her intention. Lisbeth reflected that she had left the corporation
with ten months' severance pay, in her mind "a once-in-a-lifetime
opportunity" to start a business and make a profit. She had achieved
her goal in eleven months. "I didn't know if I could do it," she said. "I
just knew what I had to do. If my plan would yield to hard work, I
would succeed, and if it wouldn't, I would figure it out."

On her journey to develop a "self-employed" attitude, Lisbeth
learned that "the fear was far worse than the reality of getting it done."
In the corporation, she had been seen as hard to manage and

overzealous. But as a sole proprietor, she found that these qualities were seen as two of her strengths. Reframed as assets in her current work, "hard to manage" is a code phrase for her creativity and "overzealous" simply means that she does not accept "no." She is a specialist at looking for ways to get a "yes." In her line of work, she is paid to secure coverage for her clients with the financial media.

Lisbeth plans never again to join a large organization. She feels she is unable to do her best work in that setting. "I chose to work from home," she stated. "I work and tend my garden. My garden is a metaphor for being in touch with and in charge of my life. Solely to work is not me; I want a lifestyle." Lisbeth has given herself permission to listen to and act on her independent and risk-taking personality. Now she chooses the people with whom she works, as well as her salary, hours, and benefits.

Every day, Lisbeth works for her independence and to satisfy her clients. She noted, "I can make all the money I need in less than forty hours per week." During the rest of the time, she does volunteer work, supporting others; spends time with her children and friends; and enjoys the outdoors, especially tending her garden and walking.

Early-Retired or Never-Want-to-Retire Workers

Vincent Calia
Licensed Psychologist and Health Care Provider
Former Professor of Counselor Education
    at Rhode Island College

Vincent negotiated with Rhode Island College and was granted "educational leave"—he will be paid but will not teach—for his last semester as a professor at the college. This arrangement will give him a financial cushion to make a transition from professor to clinician.

Vincent wants to continue to give to others by maintaining his psychotherapy practice; he also wants to enjoy other parts of his life. At sixty-eight, why not retire? In Vincent's words, "I have something special to give to others; I feel I have talent to give, and I want to be involved in giving it as long as I can. I enjoy my practice." Vincent informs his clients intellectually and emotionally. He is excited when they reconstruct their lives—talk and act positively.

He expresses a "self-employed" attitude by choosing to do work that is meaningful to him and to others in his life. "I maintain my sense of who I am, 'a professional helper,' " said Vincent, "and I make a social contribution as I continue my practice." His practice gives continuity to his clients' lives and to his own. To support his desire for continuity and learning, Vincent also attends workshops and seminars.

When I asked him, "What do you give to others?", he answered, "Unconditional acceptance, safety—my clients can trust me—spontaneity, skill and knowledge, inventiveness, genuine caring, and my own acceptance of self." As Vincent gets older, he feels more liberated to give of himself to his clients—freely and with a sense of commitment—independently and interdependently.

Judith Obermayer

Consultant to Early-Stage Businesses

Obermayer Associates

Judith's personal changes are reflected in the story of her career. "I have been reincarnated several times," she remarked. As Judith told her story, I counted at least five life/career changes. She began her career as a mathematics teacher at Wellesley College, then raised her children and concurrently volunteered at community groups. Next she worked as a researcher doing studies for the Small Business Administration,

where her focus was to answer the question, "What can the government do to support the development of high-technology companies?"
At the time, these companies had proved their ability to innovate, but
public policy was not a positive influence on their growth and success.
Doing research was clearly an important function, but, Judith realized,
"It did not utilize my talents fully." Her experience and self-assessment
led her to her current role as a business consultant and to the creation
of Obermayer Associates.

Judith provides an outside perspective to people in emerging businesses and helps them to analyze what their situation is and how they
will achieve their goals. These businesses span a variety of industries,
including specialty chemicals, drug-delivery systems, multimedia and
CD ROM, and telecommunications. "I look at the whole business and
its various parts," Judith said. "One part is financial management, but
there are also these essential questions: 'Is the business right for the
owner?' and 'Is what the business produces relevant to what the market
needs?'" She also noted, "Every business has a personality and culture
of its own. I coach owners to respect their own personality." The following questions, as Judith learned, are primary to one's "self-
employed" attitude: "What skills do you have to bring and which do
you *want* to bring to the marketplace?" and "Are these the skills that a
customer will buy?" Every individual, to live this attitude, must respect
his or her own personality.

Judith believes that all of her experiences have contributed to what
she is currently doing and that what she is doing now will contribute
to her future choices and ongoing journey. She commented, "A crucial
aspect of my development has been my volunteer work. People
undervalue the experience and the training they receive working as
volunteers. With the League of Women Voters, I learned budgeting,

administrating, fundraising, and public speaking. I knew I had gained confidence and expertise as a public speaker, for example, when I stated my opinion in front of 3,000 people at a League meeting."

When I asked Judith, "What about retirement?", there was dead silence. She at last responded, "I've turned another corner—toward mentoring minority- and woman-owned businesses. I grew up as a mathematician; I was before my time and I fought my battles, but these battles should not have been issues. Still, I don't think many women business owners get their fair shake. I'm trying to work to make this society equitable toward women."

Judith is always engaged in a self-awareness process. She asks herself (and her clients), "What is really important to me at this point?" She commented, "My passion changes over time. I can't imagine not being busy. When things let up, I find something else to involve myself in. Remaining alert and vigorous means staying involved. One of my role models was my father-in-law, a practicing attorney into his nineties. He was ninety-eight when he died. My mother is also involved. She is active in a personal sense; she is eighty-five."

For individuals, Judith believes a "self-employed" attitude means to "stay involved," and for organizations, it means "empowering workers, listening to their suggestions, and watching them grow and perform better."

Leo F. Johnson
Adult Learning Specialist

At the age of sixty-four, Leo continues to rearrange his career. He has four "jobs": coach to adult learners; field faculty/mentor at the Fielding Institute; organizational consultant in the areas of conflict, negotiation, and stress; and part-owner of a family farm in western Kansas, where he grew up.

Two early life experiences significantly shaped Leo's career, his values and attitudes, and his fortitude. When he was five years old, he nearly died of dust pneumonia. Leo commented, "In the early 1930s, on the plains of Kansas, there were days on end of stirred-up dust. It was like a blizzard, as though we were having six weeks of snow. The dust got in my lungs." The other incident occurred when Leo was seventeen; then he almost died of rheumatic fever, a viral infection that affects the heart. "In both instances," Leo said, "my great-grandmother saved me. She was there for me and nursed me back to health." Today Leo has a mission—the same one he has had throughout his life: "to look out for others because someone looked out for me." Leo asserted, "My life is a gift. When you're given a gift, I believe you have to share it."

Leo went off to school to fulfill his father's wishes, to become an accountant and return to the farm. But as he experienced life on campus and listened to his heart, Leo decided he wanted to counsel other students. His passion—to look out for others—later led him to enter a seminary, where he was ordained as a campus minister. With wisdom and zeal, Leo worked with the YMCA and at campus ministries, such as those at Northwestern University and North Dakota State. At Boston University, he earned his doctorate in adult learning, and at the Boston YMCA, he became director of the university department providing campus ministry services to many of the major colleges in the Boston area. His work involved organizing adult learning programs (student unions, dormitory services), seminars, discussions, and work-study and volunteer projects. "Throughout my career," Leo remarked, "I have done for others that which I have done for myself. I have helped people to free themselves up to learn, to feel good about learning, learning about themselves and the world."

Leo added, "Along in my career, I was mentored." Malcolm Knowles, the father of adult education, guided and encouraged Leo while he studied at Boston University and worked at the Boston YMCA. John Crystal, one of the founders of the life/work planning movement (Richard Bolles is the other), helped Leo focus on "what he really enjoyed." Leo discovered what he most enjoyed: the adult learning process, supporting others, being curious, and working with groups and organizations. He continues to express his "self-employed" attitude today—with enthusiasm, wisdom, and zeal. Leo exclaimed, "There is little I do that I don't enjoy!"

Recent College Graduates

Elisabeth Drumm

Sales Associate

Ziff-Davis Publishing

In 1991, Elisabeth Drumm graduated from Hobart and William Smith College with a liberal arts degree in French literature. She answered a newspaper advertisement and three weeks after graduation got a job with the Boston-based division of Ziff-Davis, publishers of computer magazines. During a two-year period at Ziff-Davis, Elizabeth developed a dedication to the company—she believed in what it did—fine-tuned some of her skills, learned about the world of work, and became *clear* about her next career/life move.

Inspired by the belief that "if you can live and succeed in New York City, you can do well anywhere," Elisabeth decided to move there. Although she had been successful working as a sales assistant and secretary and she had the respect of her boss in Boston, she was dissatisfied with the status quo. In her words, "I had the drive and was willing to be open to new experiences." Elisabeth wanted to stay with the same company, but she wanted to get closer to the heart of the sales organization. Her goal was to become a salesperson, and the New York headquarters was the place to do that.

On examining her background and reviewing her existing network, Elisabeth found a match. She had a contact in the Ziff-Davis international sales division, where she felt her recent studies in French literature would be most applicable. As luck would have it, the timing was right and her contact informed her of a job opening as a sales assistant. Elisabeth got the job and moved to New York City.

There were no guarantees; six months after taking the job in the international division, Elisabeth heard rumblings that her job, along with others, might be eliminated. Rather than waiting for the boom to drop, she scheduled a meeting with a human resources representative. Elisabeth informed the representative that she was dedicated to Ziff-Davis and would like to be considered for a "sales associate" position, a step up, should her job be eliminated. Today Elisabeth is working as a sales associate, prospecting clients and writing proposals.

Elisabeth felt that a big part of a "self-employed" attitude is "trusting yourself." She continued, "If you want to stay in the same company, you've got to put effort into staying. I had an inner knowing about what to do and a strong desire to move to a new place and start a new job."

Matthew Miller
Communications Marketing Specialist
Thomson and Thomson

During a six-month job search following graduation, Matthew adopted "self-employed" ways of thinking: He let go of any notions of what a job search entails and learned to be flexible, to research, and to network. As a result, he landed his first full-time job at Thomson and Thomson, trademark and copyright research authorities.

Matthew commented, "I developed a system of building blocks that led me to my job." Unlike the interlocking blocks that so many parents and children are familiar with today, Matthew's didn't stack so neatly. In the beginning of his search, as many job seekers also expect, Matthew had imagined that his first job would be full-time and that employers would be more receptive than they were to his superior grade point average and school accomplishments—as though graduation led to guaranteed employment. Before he was hired at Thomson and Thomson, Matthew held several jobs: driving a school bus part-time, writing freelance advertising copy for a bicycle manufacturer, and selling parts in a motorcycle shop—building blocks that at first glance didn't quite stack up to Matthew's expectations and hopes.

Just as I recommend that my clients do, Matthew took time to identify his skills and interests. His degree was in English; his core skills were researching, organizing, and writing; and he had an interest in journalism and advertising. In addition, Matthew's hobbies were motocross and trail biking. "Working freelance and in the motorcycle shop gave me an opportunity to explore my hobbies occupationally. It would have been a mistake not to have had these experiences," Matthew admitted. "I was getting valuable work experience, and I earned some money. My experiences led me to my current job."

When Matthew interviewed with Thomson and Thomson, he felt confident because his portfolio reflected the range of his experience and expertise. He also benefited from the practice he had had interviewing for other jobs. "Not only," said Matthew, "did they ask me questions about the relevancy of my background to their needs, but I also questioned them. I asked, for example, 'What provisions do you make for the ongoing education of your workers?' and 'How much room for creativity will I have in this job?' " Matthew's questions gave him a sense of a company's values and gave the employer exposure to his.

Matthew has this advice for college graduates who choose to adopt a "self-employed" attitude: "Don't be afraid to do work for free to show companies your value. You may have to freelance or work part-time at first, just to get a foot in the door. This is a stressful and uncertain part of the process, but it is necessary. Remember, you're in this for the long run, so stick with it!"

Michael Hale

Chemist

Yale University

Michael received his Ph.D. in organic chemistry from Boston College in January 1994. He is now working as a postdoctorate student, a paid, nonacademic position at Yale University.

After working for four years as a research assistant in the biotechnology industry, Michael learned that he had little control over the kind of work he was doing. He mused, "My ideas were rarely listened to. I was following others' thoughts." Michael decided that he wanted to do his own research, a decision requiring that he go back to school. It was a long road. As Michael reported, "I went to school for eleven years. It's been a big investment and a long-term solution to have control of my work. I traded off free time, time with my wife and friends, earning a living, and nice vacations."

Michael expressed a "self-employed" attitude by demonstrating his flexibility and staying true to his long-term vision. In the beginning, he tried pursuing his Ph.D. by going to school at night and working during the day. He discovered both required a full-time commitment.

Michael's desire to become a Ph.D. chemist was inspired by his maternal grandparents, who were both chemists. He chose to attend school full-time. "I've taken this avenue," Michael stated, "because I enjoy the work, it's fun, and I like making progress—completing things. Unlike fields such as law, medicine, and finance, where formal schooling ends with a clear graduation date, in my field, chemistry," Michael added, "there is no time frame. I haven't been sure when I would graduate. I thought that I would finish in November, but my adviser made the arbitrary decision that I would graduate in January." I asked Michael, "With this type of ambiguity added to the long-term nature of your program, plus some of the tradeoffs you've made, how did you keep on going?" Michael answered, "I invested in something that I really believe in." Apt advice for all.

Other Workers

Joyce Copland

Writer-Editor, Work/Family Directions, Inc.

President, Copland & Company

As a former vice-president of marketing at Addison-Wesley Publishing Company, Joyce said, "I was on a classic career ladder where I rose quickly. I had a terrific job, earning plenty of money, and no life. I was exhausted all the time." Today, as the mother of a twelve-year-old, she has redesigned her career/life.

To make a 360-degree shift, Joyce readily admitted that she was supported economically: "I have a gainfully employed spouse who has a health care program." But, she stated, "I'm the one who recognized that my life wasn't working and agonized about the decisions I needed to make. I took time off to think about what I really wanted to do with my life. I decided having a 'good' job where I made a lot of money was not my primary value."

Adopting a "self-employed" attitude has its price. Joyce said, "I gave up pursuing options that opened up immediate opportunities." The fast track! She struggled with giving up her prestigious job, generous income, and role identity. Instead, she made "a life choice," in her words, "that gives me freedom—time to know my family, time to know something else besides work."

As a writer-editor at Work/Family Directions, Inc., Joyce agreed to a "telecommuter" work relationship. Work/Family Directions is a Boston-based consultancy that manages worker resource programs for corporate clients (IBM, AT&T) and helps workers manage work/family concerns. As a telecommuter, Joyce drives to the office at Work/Family Directions once or twice a week and works from 7:30 A.M. to 3:30 P.M; this schedule helps her to avoid rush hours. For the remainder of the week, she works from her home office, where she does put in about eight hours per day, but not necessarily from nine to five. She balances work, family, and personal needs. Joyce's responsibility is to deliver a certain amount of valued work. Work/Family Directions believes that she will be a more productive worker if her attention is not diverted to balancing work/family needs.

Joyce has met her needs and been able to meet others' needs by honoring four "self-employed" values that have been instrumental in guiding and directing her in her career *and* life success:

1. To have control of my time—organize my priorities the way I want.

2. To work with people I like.

3. To earn a reasonable amount of money.

4. To continue learning.

Joyce summarized, "The change I've made has given me the chance to explore and live life fully. I'd never had time to know I loved the outdoors. Now I work *and* take walks *and* volunteer at a horse farm helping disabled children ride."

Arthur
Taxi Driver

Whenever my wife, Amy, and I take a trip, we call Arthur to give us a ride to the airport. Most often, Arthur tells us stories about his life; these usually have to do with his homeland, the Middle East, or with an event associated with driving a cab.

One time, on the first leg of an excursion Amy and I were taking to Italy, Arthur told us a "cab story" about advocating for what he felt was the "right thing to do." Arthur began, "A couple of weeks ago, a driver hit my cab on purpose. The accident was clearly avoidable, but some people take advantage of the cab companies, hitting us, with the intent to collect [sue]. Most of these cases get settled out of court; the cab company's insurance company ends up paying the driver. It's unfair. I never told my boss about the accident, but when the insurance company called me, I told them, 'Just because it's not my cab company, it's still not right that the driver collect. I have a conscience, and you need to have one too. That lady hit me for selfish reasons.' "

The insurance company listened to Arthur. On further examination, it decided to contest the claim. Arthur continued, "I could have ignored the driver and let her collect, but whether I own the company is irrelevant. Her claim was founded on false grounds."

Later, as the plane took off, I turned to Amy and said, "Did you listen to Arthur's story? He has a 'self-employed' attitude!"

David D. Worth

Senior Vice-President, Marketing and Business Development

Blasland, Bouck & Lee, Inc.

David said, "I'll always remember what Ray, one of my network contacts, told me during my career transition: 'There is somebody out there who *wants* you in their organization. It is your job to find that person.'"

After twelve years with ABB Environmental Services, Inc., David resigned from his senior-level management position. "I was part of the 'new boss/new team' syndrome," David reported. "We agreed to disagree." During the course of David's tenure, the organization had several different owners, each with a different operating philosophy. Each new boss brought his or her own ideas and unique style. The fit between David and the new leaders progressively diverged. "Emotionally," David reflected, "I felt the new boss had no right—hadn't *earned* the right—to what we had developed. I had a hard time giving up what I had created. Today, though, I see that I did what I could to develop the organization. I take sole responsibility for leaving."

David's "self-employed" attitude is expressed through his deliberate efforts to learn personally and professionally and by his agility—an ability to turn his learning into action. In 1986, encouraged by his father-in-law, an executive and a proponent of intensive training programs, David took Harvard University's advanced management program. The program was a fourteen-week miniversion of a Harvard MBA. "It was rigorous and content-filled," said David. "I got a general management grounding, including marketing, finance, and operations; every year since, I get more clear on what I learned from this program. Back then, my class was 50 percent foreigners; I saw the beginnings of a world market. I saw the dedication of the foreign students; prior to entering the program, each had spent months away from home, learning English."

This program significantly contributed to David's professional learning and development. His resignation from ABB, the resultant grief, and the act of finding another meaningful job stretched him personally. David anticipated that his job would come to an end, but dealing with—really feeling—his loss took four months; then he revised his résumé. "Those four months," David reflected, "indicated I was not ready. When I did put my résumé together, I realized, 'Wow! How much I have done'; this was a watershed event."

David set up an office in his home, a practical space and an anchor, from which he conducted a diligent job search. "I looked at my search as a new course in my life," David said. "Beginning at eight o'clock most mornings, I would start contacting people in my network. I wasn't embarrassed; I got the word out that I was leaving the company and needed information about the marketplace." He chose to stay in the environmental engineering industry. And for emotional and financial reasons, he determined that he wanted to work at a company, not start a business.

Right Associates, an international outplacement firm, helped David to get further in touch with his feelings and direction. David said, "The outplacement firm had no agenda. They wanted me to get a job that was right for me. My friends, children, and wife all had an agenda; the objective guidance helped me see what was best for me."

David picked Blasland, Bouck & Lee, Inc., as his next employer, an environmental engineering and consulting firm. About his choice and the learning that came from his career transition, he now says, "I've been hired into the company; for their convenience, they have given me a title and benefits. I cannot assume that they will provide the next

step or job for me. This is my responsibility, whether I work in or outside of an organization."

One of the reasons David agreed to be interviewed was to give back
to others what was given to him. "Part of my dedication," he stated, "is
to help younger people and others to cope with their development."

Gordon MacKenzie
Self-Proclaimed "Sharer"
Gordon said, "Through role modeling, I show people it is possible to
be vulnerable and survive with grace." Gordon "shares" of himself by
giving presentations and workshops on developing and maintaining
creativity.

Before dubbing himself a sharer, Gordon worked for thirty years at
Hallmark, where he wrote and designed humor cards, sculpted wild
animals for a children's learning center, directed the creation of two
syndicated comic strips, designed three restaurants, established Hallmark's Humor Workshop, and slowly evolved into a self-styled corporate shaman.

Gordon remarked, "One of the things that drives me to have a 'self-
employed' mindset is pursuing who I am." He added, "I'm not sure
that I will ever arrive there. I respond to notions; I do not analyze or
balance pros and cons. I am driven by the excitement of bringing a
notion to fruition."

While at Hallmark, Gordon perceived that he was being "moved
out" of the company. Gordon reported, "I was being offered a nothing
job, going from senior design manager of the Humor Workshop to a
job with no title. The Humor Workshop was a creative, friendly environment for artists and writers. I asked my boss if he had a title in
mind. He said 'Aide de Camp.' This was a militaristic term that basical-

ly meant 'assistant.' " Gordon expressed his dissatisfaction, and so his boss encouraged him to come up with something else. The term *paradox* came to Gordon's mind. His job title at the time he left Hallmark in 1991 was "Creative Paradox."

Gordon expressed a "self-employed" attitude while under the corporate umbrella and continues to use the attitude in his current work as a way of self-expression—living his life and giving to others. "At the heart of being employed," Gordon commented, "is my resistance to becoming a commodity." For example, some workers at large corporations like General Motors are referred to as "units." Gordon refused to feel like, be seen as, or see others as a unit. In his role as Creative Paradox, Gordon developed exercises for unblocking creative energy; he designed a corporate Merlin's den. His personal journey includes the lesson that no one can afford to "piddle away" his or her integrity. As a sharer, he expands and extends his *real* self and the creative oasis he developed at Hallmark to individuals and organizations throughout the world.

◪

**You always plant your feet firmly on the ground
if you want to be able to jump up in the air.**

—*Joan Miro*

The End Is the Beginning

Early in the morning on Columbus Day 1993, I stood in front of my home in Cambridge, Massachusetts, looking across Memorial Drive to the Charles River. Suddenly, a bullet-shaped car with a one-seat cockpit sped by, followed by a vehicle with flashing lights. I guessed that the "bullet" car must have been experimental and that it was probably heading three miles up the road to its birthplace, the Massachusetts Institute of Technology (MIT).

"How appropriate," I thought, "that on our holiday for celebrating 'discovery,' innovators are pioneering and testing a new and unusual vehicle." I imagined that the experimental car was a result of a team effort and that each of the inventors had courage, imagination, and a spirit of adventure. Each had taken on a responsibility to invent something new—to "discover" and test a different way of doing something. And most likely, as my grandfather had, the inventors had each challenged conventional wisdom—their own and others'.

Like the flock of geese, a team of individuals (independent) had come together for a common purpose (interdependent). While watching this car on its test run, I saw the initial result of a collective effort. Someday, you may be buying the final result of that effort!

The inventors work independently, *with* MIT and *with* one another. It is amazing what individuals can do when their intention is clear, they know themselves, and they take responsibility for harnessing individual and team energy. They overcome inner and outer obstacles and persevere to make what they have imagined a reality. As a result, like Christopher Columbus and my grandfather, they work authentically, collaboratively, and productively—from their passion. They are discovering new frontiers and stretching beyond what others may never have thought was humanly possible. They are burning the grass. My grandfather passed his "self-employed" attitude on to me. I am offering a "self-employed" attitude—a new social contract—for all.

Notes

Introduction

1. For an in-depth look at these issues, please refer to my book *When You Lose Your Job* (San Francisco: Berrett-Koehler, 1993).

2. Charles Handy, *The Age of Unreason* (Boston: Harvard Business School Press, 1989), 178.

Chapter 1: Beginning the Process of Change with Yourself

1. Rollo May, *The Art of Counseling* (Nashville, Tenn.: Abingdon, 1993), 152.

2. John J. Keller and Gautam Naik, "US West to Cut 9,000 Positions, Take Big Charge," *Wall Street Journal*, September 20, 1993, A3.

3. Peter Block, *Stewardship: Choosing Service over Self-Interest* (San Francisco: Berrett-Koehler, 1993), 33.

Chapter 2: Facing the Dragon—Your Work Fears

1. Carlos Castaneda, *The Fire from Within* (New York: Simon and Schuster, 1984).

Chapter 3: Integrating Independence and Interdependence

1. Harry Levinson, *The Great Jackass Fallacy* (Cambridge, Mass.: Harvard University Press, 1973), 10.

Chapter 4: Joining, Not Working for, Your Organization and Customers

1. Jack Welch, "Jack Welch's Lessons for Success," *Fortune*, January 25, 1993, 92.

2. Michael P. Cronin, "One Life to Love," *Inc.*, July 1993, 60, 63. Other workplaces employees love are cited on pages 57, 66, 70, and 73.

3. Sue Shellenbarger, "Work-Force Study Finds Loyalty Is Weak, Divisions of Race and Gender Are Deep," *Wall Street Journal*, September 3, 1993, 1.

Chapter 5: Committing to Continuous Learning

1. Angles Arrien, "The Bridge of Healing: Discovering the Universal Themes of Human Culture," *Magical Blend*, October 1990, 92–94.

2. Rollo May, *Man's Search for Himself* (New York: W. W. Norton, 1953), 33.

3. May, *Man's Search for Himself*, 21.

4. Shawn Tully, "Your Paycheck Gets Exciting," *Fortune*, November 1, 1993, 83.

Chapter 6: Creating Meaningful Work

1. Quoted in Andrea Higgins, "Tranquility through Balance," *Beverly Times*, April 28, 1993, A5.

Index

The Author

CLIFF HAKIM (pronounced Ha-*keem*) is a career and work consultant, specializing in self-leadership and rethinking work. Cliff believes the world counts on each of us to become a leader. He is dedicated to guiding individuals inside and outside of organizations through change that results in personal enhancement and gratification, and organization/customer relevant work.

Cliff customizes Rethinking Work[SM] seminars and presentations for corporations, professional service firms, universities and asssociations. In addition, he develops other methods and implements other strategies for supporting and developing self-leadership inside and outside of organizations. Organizational clients include Bull HN Information Systems, T. J. Maxx, the Boston Company, the Boston Financial Group, John F. Kennedy University, Worcester Polytechnic Institute, Assumption College and the New England Banking Institute. Individual clients include professionals and managers at all levels, from partners in an advertising agency to human resource managers to individual entrepreneurs to corporate executives, who are seeking guidance in clarifying their needs and purpose, and creating more satisfying and relevant work.

Cliff's writing has enabled him to reach a broader audience with stories, information and tools that can influence and change their lives. His first book is *When You Lose Your Job* (Berrett-Koehler, 1993). *We Are All Self-Employed* (Berrett-Koehler, 1994) is his second book.

Through dozens of real-life examples, it supports and teaches people in learning how to let go of a dependent mindset and live from the perspective of taking responsibility for their own careers inside or outside of organizations. *We Are All Self-Employed* was selected by *Industry Week* as one of the top ten management books of 1994. As well, *We Are All Self-Employed* was chosen by the Institute for Management Studies (IMS) as their June 1995 book-of-the-month selection. This book was sent by IMS to over four hundred Fortune 500 sponsoring member companies.

Cliff earned his master's degree in special education from Boston College and has done postgraduate work in human and organizational development at the Fielding Institute. For Cliff, practicing self-leadership is a daily, life-long endeavor.

The author welcomes your comments and conversation and invites you to contact him at Hakim and Company, Harvard Square, 50 Church Street, Cambridge, MA 02138, 617–661–1250 (fax 617–868–3462).